COCONUT OIL
NATURE'S PERFECT INGREDIENT

OVER 100 RECIPES INCLUDING HEALTHY DISHES
AND BAKED TREATS TO NURTURE YOUR BODY AND
BEAUTY IDEAS TO FEED YOUR SKIN

Lucy Bee

QUADRILLE

Photography by Ria Osborne

PUBLISHING DIRECTOR Sarah Lavelle
COMMISSIONING EDITOR Lisa Pendreigh
COPY EDITOR Sally Somers
CREATIVE DIRECTOR Helen Lewis
ART DIRECTION AND DESIGN Katherine Keeble
ASSISTANT DESIGNER Emily Lapworth
PHOTOGRAPHER Ria Osborne
FOOD STYLIST Emily Jonzen
PROPS STYLIST Holly Bruce
PRODUCTION DIRECTOR Vincent Smith
PRODUCTION CONTROLLER Emily Noto

First published in 2015 by
Quadrille Publishing Limited

Text © 2015 Lucy Bee Ltd
Photography © 2015 Ria Osborne
Design and layout © 2015
Quadrille Publishing Ltd

Quadrille is an imprint of Hardie Grant
www.hardiegrant.com.au

Quadrille Publishing Ltd
Pentagon House
52–54 Southwark Street
London SE1 1UN
www.quadrille.co.uk

Reprinted in 2015
10 9 8 7 6 5 4 3 2

Cataloguing in Publication Data: a
catalogue record for this book is available
from the British Library.

ISBN: 978 1 84949 675 9

Printed in Italy

FSC
www.fsc.org

MIX
Paper from
responsible sources
FSC® C008047

COCONUT OIL: NATURE'S PERFECT INGREDIENT

When I first sat down to write this book, I spent hours trawling through my recipes so that I could bring you a collection of the most delicious – yet healthy – foods imaginable. I've included extra preparation or cooking tips wherever I can, with key allergy advice for each recipe. On pages 184–189 you will find an outline of the nutritional and health benefits of the ingredients I use most often. I hope that, with this book as a guide and a jar of coconut oil to hand, you'll be able to transform your eating regime. However busy your week gets, with these recipes you'll always be able to find enough time to eat healthily.

'THE KITCHEN IS THE HEART OF OUR HOME. FOOD IS THERE TO BE ENJOYED.'

One of the questions I am always being asked is how Lucy Bee coconut oil came to be. Well, the story behind us is quite simple, really – our approach is all about eating unprocessed, fresh, organic foods, where possible. This means our food is as close to nature as we can make it.

I've spent my life having to scan labels and check ingredients. I was diagnosed as coeliac when I was just 18 months old, and back then there were hardly any pre-prepared gluten-free foods on the shelves. Right from my diagnosis, my parents decided that as a family we should all eat the same food, which meant most of our food was cooked from scratch. Years later, we see this as a blessing in disguise because it means we've always eaten healthy, nutritious meals. Throughout our healthy journey, our vegetable patch has proven to be invaluable, and we're fortunate enough to have a seemingly endless supply of free-range organic eggs from our six chickens.

Along the way, my parents also taught me how to become a master at adapting recipes. I learned how to make pretty much anything gluten-free, while keeping it tasty, nutritious and appealing to the eye. The kitchen is the heart of our home, and I love nothing more

'AS A STABLE FAT, COCONUT OIL DOESN'T CHANGE ITS PROPERTIES WHEN HEATED.'

than getting together with friends or family to share stories of our week over a delicious meal. I hope that this book will encourage you to do the same – after all, food is there to be enjoyed.

SO, HOW DID WE DISCOVER THE WONDER THAT IS LUCY BEE COCONUT OIL?

Well, believe it or not, it all began with a humble egg...

An old family friend, Indra, sent some coconut oil and the book *The Coconut Oil Miracle* by Bruce Fife to us, all the way from Hong Kong. Indra had been raving about this incredible oil and, after reading Bruce's book, we soon realised that it was the missing piece in our jigsaw – finally, we'd found a healthy oil for cooking.

But how does the egg fit in, I hear you ask? Well, the first thing my mum ever cooked with our new jar of coconut oil was a fried egg. As she dished us up her little experiment, she waited for one of the family to complain about how our eggs tasted. However, I didn't even notice, and nor did my dad, sister and brother. And so began our family journey of cooking with coconut oil.

This was back in 2007 when unrefined coconut oil was almost unheard of and even more difficult and expensive to buy than it is now. Undeterred, we were passionate about sharing our newfound wonder cooking product with the world, so my dad set about finding ways of importing quality coconut oil at an affordable price. Eventually, Lucy Bee Ltd was founded and we began our quest to

source the very best extra virgin, organic, raw coconut oil on the planet.

Coconut oils taste different depending on the raw materials and extraction methods used, as well as the country that the coconut trees are grown in – a bit like wines, really.

We not only wanted our coconut oil be the best for quality, taste and price, but it also had to be a Fair Trade certified product, too: After all, we thought it was only right that the lives of the farmers and workers who produce our oil should be improved, as generally coconuts are grown in underprivileged areas.

Our choice of oil also had to be as natural as possible to maintain maximum nutritional benefits. So it was (and remains to this day) a very conscious decision that Lucy Bee coconut oil should be Fair Trade, extra virgin, raw and organic.

WHY ARE THE FATS IN COCONUT OIL GOOD FOR US?

For this part, I need to put on my science hat, so try not to switch off! As a nation, we're starting to realise more and more that sugars are our enemy in the obesity crisis, not fats. We need fats for fuel and they are crucial for our health, although it's important that we eat the right kinds to really maximise the efficiency of our body.

Coconut oil is a saturated fat, made up of medium-chain fatty acids (MCFAs). All fats are made up of chains, and the length of the chain just determines how the body breaks it down and uses it. The body deals with medium-chain saturated fats incredibly efficiently, and there's a wealth of research to show just how easily MCFAs are digested, metabolised and converted to ketones. Coconut oil also happens to be rich in lauric acid (in fact, it's around 48% lauric acid), also found in breast milk and full of health-boosting qualities. It gets turned into monolaurin, which is both antiviral and antibacterial. Finally, as a stable fat, coconut oil doesn't change its properties when heated, which makes it perfect for frying or roasting foods.

So, now you've heard all the good stuff, where do you start? And how much coconut oil should you be eating? Well, there isn't a set amount that you should eat each day, although I would say to aim for between 1 and 3 tablespoons used to replace existing processed oils – as with everything in life, balance is the key.

WHAT EXACTLY IS COCONUT OIL?
It may seem obvious, but coconut oil is extracted from coconut flesh, which is known as the coconut kernel. However, there are different types of coconut oil – refined and unrefined – and it's worth knowing the difference if, like me, you prefer to eat natural foods.

Refined coconut oil will be heavily processed, although it makes up about 90% of the coconut oil on the world market. Unrefined oils, like our Lucy Bee, are natural, unprocessed and extracted from a more expensive raw material.

The processed version has to be heavily refined to make it fit for human consumption. The oil gets taken from dried copra, which is then turned into crude coconut oil – a completely different oil to virgin or extra virgin coconut oil. Often, coconuts used for copra will be split in the field with an axe and chunks of coconut flesh collected and taken to a dryer. The dryer can range from solar or even a sophisticated kiln, to a simple rack over a smoky fire. Next, the copra gets bagged up, although by the time it reaches a large-scale industrial oil-seed mill (sometimes overseas and taking months) it is often rancid and mouldy. The oil that's extracted from this is a brown colour, so it is bleached white as well as deodorised.

'THE COCONUT TASTE OF THE OIL TENDS TO GET LOST WHEN YOU COOK WITH IT.'

The virgin or extra virgin coconut oil process couldn't be more different. It is extracted from the flesh of fresh, mature coconuts within 1–4 hours of the coconut being opened and is naturally white in colour. It also has a distinctly coconutty aroma and taste, although this differs depending on the country it comes from and how the oil has been extracted:

✦ Cold pressed extraction is where the oil is extracted from the dried flesh. Our oil from the Solomon Islands and the Dominican Republic are cold pressed by hand.

✦ Centrifuge extraction is where the flesh is first made into coconut milk and the oil is separated from this in a centrifuge.

When I first started using coconut oil, I didn't really notice the difference in taste. Yet, the more I ate – and I eat a lot – the more I became aware of the huge variations. Some oils are quite subtle, whereas others have a more pronounced flavour. What I always find

'WE BELIEVE IN ORGANIC FARMING AND EATING FOODS AS CLOSE TO NATURE AS POSSIBLE.'

amazing is that the coconut taste tends to get lost when you cook with it. This means that coconut oil newbies can stop worrying – you shouldn't end up with a coconut-flavoured version of all your favourite foods! As much as I go nuts for coconuts, even I wouldn't want that.

The next step after extraction is to package up the coconut oil to be sold in supermarkets and health food shops across the world. The oils will be solid at temperatures below 24°C, so in cooler climates, such as the UK, it's solid for most of the year, and in hot countries, such as the Philippines, it is sold as liquid. However, the nutrients and health benefits in the oils are not affected by melting and solidifying.

LUCY BEE EXTRA VIRGIN FAIR TRADE ORGANIC RAW COCONUT OIL

We had great fun taking our time as we tried and tested oils from all over the world. During our quest, we came across oils that we just didn't like at all. However great the companies were to deal with, if it wasn't right, it had to be: 'No, not that one.' You see, we only wanted to bring you the very best, and this led us to our first coconut oil, which comes from the Philippines. I think our oil has a delicious and delicate coconut flavour. As well as taste and aroma, we had a few other boxes to tick – things that, for us, were a must-have for our oils. Our jars of Lucy Bee had to be:

✦ **Organic:** We firmly believe in organic farming and in eating foods as close to

nature as possible. This also packs in extra nutritional value, so organic was, for us at least, a no-brainer!

✦ **Extra virgin:** When you're looking at coconut oil, virgin and extra virgin mean the same thing. It basically means that the oil is unrefined and unprocessed, which is crucial to our brand.

✦ **Raw:** This means that very little heat has been used during the extraction process – it will go no higher than 45°C. As raw foodies will tell you, this means that it retains its maximum nutritional benefits.

✦ **Fair Trade:** While the oil is the same whether it's Fair Trade certified or not, being Fair Trade certified lay at the very foundation of our company. We're passionate about making a difference to the lives of our producers, including the workers, the farmers, their families – everyone!

✦ **Glass jars:** Have you ever seen those haunting images of whales washed up on the beach, their stomachs stuffed with plastic? Our horror at seeing those forced us to question the amount of plastic that had wormed its way into our lives. And on top of that are the health implications of plastic toxins leaching into the oil. So we insist on using recyclable glass jars to package and store our oil. The jars are easy to reuse or recycle, which is much better for the environment.

To make it even easier to reuse your jars, we've even come up with an easy-peel label. In the office, we're always competing with one another, coming up with new ideas on how to reuse the jars – our larder at home is full of Lucy Bee jars holding green tea, homemade spices and pasta. My mum is a dab hand at finding uses for them, and they can even be used as flower vases or candle holders!

But back to the coconut oil itself. It's important to remember that whatever the country of origin, Lucy Bee is always raw and cold-press extracted from fresh, mature, organically grown coconuts.

FAIR TRADE – WE CAN ALL MAKE A DIFFERENCE

If I'm honest, when I was at school and was taught about Fair Trade, I didn't quite get it. I understood about the workers being paid more, of course, but had no idea of the true impact or importance of this. I genuinely didn't know that choosing a Fair Trade certified product could really make such a difference to someone's life. We pay an additional 10% to have Fair Trade oil. Of this, 70% is used for higher wages and 30% for sustainable community projects. Lucy Bee then pays 0.75% of turnover to our Fair Trade certifier, Fair Trade Sustainability Alliance (FairTSA), to help them fund their good works. In the words of Winfried Fuchshofen, FairTSA Director: 'We will all continue our path to supporting a fairer world for all, creating new possibilities and living conditions for rural communities around the globe.'

Since we launched, Lucy Bee's Fair Trade premium has helped to pay for two wells in the Philippines to bring clean, fresh water to rural villages. Before this, the women had to trek for two miles to fetch water, so you can imagine the difference that this has made to their everyday lives. Thanks to you, our customers, we've also helped to buy solar light bulbs for the villagers' small, one-roomed wooden homes, and we've even funded scholarships for education. Over in the Solomon Islands, our Fair Trade contributions have paid for everyday benefits, such as medicine and education and here, too, solar bulbs have replaced dangerous kerosene lamps. In the Dominican Republic, our Fair Trade contributions help provide work for abandoned single mothers. They make a huge difference to the lives of individuals and whole villages.

Seeing all this happen in the first couple of years was a real eye opener. It's an amazing feeling to know that when you are buying Lucy Bee coconut oil, you are not only changing your lifestyle into a healthier one, but also improving someone else's life, somewhere in the world. A great feeling, right?

And knowing about Fair Trade has encouraged me to always look for the logo on goods when I'm shopping – bananas, chocolate, coffee, and everything I can. Sometimes these foods may cost a few extra pence, but it's really worth it when you think about the lives they'll change. I have also been encouraged to consider where our food comes from. As well as looking at ingredients, it's good to support local producers and farmers' markets wherever possible. For me, the quality of ingredients, the packaging, production methods and the ethics behind a food are every bit as important as the taste.

'WHEN BUYING LUCY BEE COCONUT OIL, YOU'RE NOT ONLY CHANGING YOUR LIFESTYLE TO A HEALTHIER ONE, BUT ALSO IMPROVING SOMEONE ELSE'S LIFE.'

So, you've bought the book and got your jar of Lucy Bee, but what can you actually do with it? Well, I bet that in no time at all you'll be as hooked as I am on this one, versatile jar of what I like to call 'the miracle oil'. However, you'll probably mostly use our Lucy Bee as a fantastic, natural oil, or a replacement for processed vegetable oils and butter.

COOKING WITH COCONUT OIL

It's perfect for frying foods such as eggs, onions, garlic, meats or fish, and, honestly, you only need to use a teeny amount. I don't know why, but a little most definitely goes a long way. Lucy Bee is ideal for roasting, too. You can smear it over meats or fish and toss your vegetables in it, all with wonderful results. If you like the sound of this, then you should definitely check out our recipe for Roast Potatoes page 118 – a real winner in our house on Sundays.

You'll also be able to use coconut oil as a replacement for butter in baking, which is great news if you are lactose intolerant. Because Lucy Bee seems to go further, I find using 25% less than the recommend amount of butter called for in a recipe works just fine. It also has a special kind of sweetness that means you will be able to cut down on the sugar in the recipe by a third, making your cakes instantly healthier! Amazingly though, savoury recipes won't be made to taste sweet – instead, the coconut oil simply enhances the flavours, and the coconut flavour is often lost when you cook with it. You can use Lucy Bee as a spread instead of butter, which tastes great on rice cakes or toast. If you decide to try this there is definitely a hint of a coconut

taste, but it works well with jams, marmite, or nut butters.

Our wonderful followers on social media also introduced me to Bulletproof coffee (see page 43), which is espresso whizzed with Lucy Bee and grass-fed butter. If you haven't tried this, you must give it a go! It's the ultimate homemade latte and tastes utterly delicious. Whenever somebody new tries it, they can't

'WHEREVER YOU WOULD USE OIL OR BUTTER IN COOKING, GO AHEAD AND SUBSTITUTE WITH LUCY BEE.'

get their head around the fact that it hasn't got any milk in it.

You could also try adding a teaspoon of Lucy Bee to smoothies for extra nourishment, and I even stir a teaspoon into my daily cup of green tea – it tastes just perfect, and if you're not a fan of green tea, adding Lucy Bee makes it taste so much better. Plus, it leaves your lips feeling super soft. How often do you get a drink and lip balm all in one?

While that may seem a whole lot of uses for just one jar, I guess that the simple answer to 'How do you use coconut oil?' is this: wherever you would use an oil or butter in cooking, just go ahead and substitute with Lucy Bee.

'I FEEL SO MUCH BETTER WHEN I EAT THE MOST NATURAL, NOURISHING INGREDIENTS POSSIBLE.'

EATING AS NATURE INTENDED

As already mentioned, being coeliac meant that I had to grow up studying ingredients in all food products, but I know that I feel so much better when I eat the most natural, nourishing ingredients possible. In each of the recipes you read in this book, I recommend that you use organic, unprocessed ingredients – the foods that nature intended – wherever you can. I also prefer to use good-quality, grass-fed meats as I believe not only in the ethos that 'we are what we eat', but that 'we are whatever we eat has eaten!'

People often ask me if I use other oils, and the answer is yes! As much as I love using Lucy Bee, there's still a place in my kitchen cupboards for good-quality extra virgin olive oil to whip up delicious dressings. I also especially like Udo's oil, as a fabulous source of healthy oils.

Because of my intolerance to gluten, my recipes are always gluten-free, but please don't feel you have to do the same.

GROW YOUR OWN

At home, we've always been fortunate enough to enjoy fruit and vegetables fresh from the garden. Growing up, my siblings and I would roll our eyes and say, 'Not again!' as Mum and Dad would serve up delicious meals, telling us with each mouthful how the potatoes or onions were 'from the garden'.

It's only now I'm older (and maybe a little wiser!) that I can understand their pride. I love hearing what's growing in our garden, and knowing that the foods I'll be eating are organic and home-grown – perfect.

Growing your own vegetables is incredibly rewarding, so if you haven't tried it already,

why not have a go? You don't need to be particularly green-fingered and could just start with something easy like sprouting beans and seeds, which taste divine in salads and have incredible health benefits. You could also try some herbs, maybe, and then have fun using them in recipes. It's such an amazing feeling to cook with something that you've grown yourself.

Where possible, I also try to eat foods that are in season. At home we freeze the fruit and vegetables we have an abundance of, to enjoy later in the year. We freeze fruits such as raspberries and blackberries to make wonderful bases for crumbles or coulis, and tomato gluts can be turned into delicious sauces to store in the freezer. My parents even freeze herbs, such as parsley, ready to add to soups and stocks.

'EVERY TIME YOU EAT OR DRINK, YOU'RE EITHER FIGHTING DISEASE OR FEEDING IT.'

The other thing that's great about having a vegetable patch is that you can have your own compost heap – an ideal way of using up trimmings, peelings and leftovers, and great for fertilising.

KEEPING CHICKENS

Since our journey of using coconut oil began with a humble egg, I guess it's appropriate to mention that this same egg came from one of our own chickens. Nelson, Pepper, Saffi, Sylvia, Doris and Maggie are never happier than wandering through the vegetable patch, pecking away at their daily treat of Lucy Bee mixed in with their food. They produce the best eggs for us and, hand on heart, I can honestly say that there's nothing better than our own happy chickens' eggs cooked in Lucy Bee. I must thank them for supplying us with delicious food to enjoy every single day.

IT'S ALL ABOUT BALANCE, PLANNING AND PREPARATION

I really hope that you have fun trying out these recipes and, if you're anything like me, sharing them with your family and friends. There are few better times than a family dinner where we all catch up with what's been going on. Eating healthily is all about balance, and the same can be said about using Lucy Bee in your cooking – everything in moderation.

As you'll see in the recipes in this book, I love trying to turn unhealthy foods into healthy ones by adapting recipes with a Lucy Bee twist. My followers on social media will also know that there are times when I enjoy letting loose and indulging in particular foods. This is where adapting recipes really comes into its own, and I'll have a go at transforming pancakes or cakes, making them not only healthy, but also tasty and satisfying.

I'm sure that you don't need me to tell you that planning ahead can make a huge difference to eating well. I tend to make extra, then either freeze meals or use up spare ingredients in other recipes. Leftover sweet potatoes, for instance, are good cold in a salad, or warm in an omelette the next day – it's always a bonus to open the fridge and find leftovers that you can quickly use in another creation!

Before I leave you to read on, I thought I'd share one of my favourite quotes that pretty much sums up my philosophy for life: 'Every time you eat or drink, you're either fighting disease or feeding it.'

Happy cooking,

TIP

There are not many cooking oils that you can also use as a moisturiser, but Lucy Bee is one of them. Any leftover coconut oil on the knife or spoon, simply rub over dry skin.

ALLERGY INFORMATION

If, like me, you have a particular food intolerance then you will be forever checking packaging and labels to decipher what you can and can't eat. To make your cooking choices easier, each of the recipes in this book is accompanied by a symbol – or symbols – denoting the suitability of the dish for people following specific diets. Below is an at-a-glance guide to what each of those symbols stands for:

- Gluten-free   GF
- Wheat-free   WF
- Dairy-free   DF
- Lactose-free   LF
- Vegetarian   VEG
- Vegan   V

STORECUPBOARD STAPLES

These are my everyday essential foodstuffs – the ingredients I always have stored in the kitchen cupboards or fridge, ready for making simple, nutritious meals.

At home, we always make everything from scratch, whether it's our own sauces or even curry powders, so I've tried to include the basics for these here, too, as they can really transform your meals.

✦ **Lucy Bee coconut oil.** This is your new go-to cooking oil. If you need to soften it to use in cooking or baking, then either melt it in the oven as it preheats, or place the jar in warm water, on a radiator, Aga, or even briefly in the microwave.

✦ **Apple cider vinegar.** I love the raw, organic, unfiltered and undistilled cloudy version, which still has the 'mother of vinegar', or cloudy sediment, that contains most of the health-promoting bacterial properties.

✦ **Avocado.** These green fruits taste wonderful on their own, or use to thicken your smoothies. They're rich in antioxidants and folate, too.

✦ **Bragg Liquid Aminos.** This soy sauce alternative is full of amino acids and so tasty too.

✦ **Cacao.** While you can use unsweetened cocoa powder in recipes, cacao is much better for you as it retains all its nutrients and wonderful antioxidants. It can even send moods soaring. What's not to like?

✦ **Cinnamon.** This natural sweetener is a traditional remedy for digestive problems and tastes great added to your porridge.

✦ **Eggs.** Organic, free-range eggs are worth the extra cost, as you know what the chickens have been fed, meaning it's all free from chemicals. I hate the idea of battery hens too, so I always buy organic chicken, and would rather go without if I can't find organic.

✦ **Green tea.** I always have a cafetière on the go, full of green tea.

✦ **Healthy oils.** As well as my Lucy Bee, I keep a bottle of Udo's oil in the cupboard for endless body-loving benefits.

✦ **Himalayan pink salt.** Not all salts are equal! This pretty salt helps to balance the body's pH levels, as well as aiding nutrient absorption.

✦ **Nuts.** Brazils, cashews, walnuts, pecans and almonds are all brilliantly healthy and versatile. Their oils are especially beneficial.

✦ **Seaweeds.** These are great to throw into meals and cooking as they're high in calcium, can alkalise the body and can even purify the blood.

✦ **Seeds.** I use all sorts of seeds, from pumpkin to sunflower and chia. Try sprouting alfalfa seeds, so easy to do and wonderfully healthy. They make a lovely topping for dishes or filling in sandwiches.

✦ **Spices.** Keep a range, ideally buying them whole and then grinding them yourself in a nut and seed or even coffee grinder, for fresh and cheaper blends. If you make too much of any spice mix, store any extra in your empty Lucy Bee jars.

ESSENTIAL EQUIPMENT

As well as fully-stocked kitchen cupboards, a range of equipment makes preparing food easier. My must-haves include:

✦ **Sugar alternatives.** I love stevia, agave nectar, maple syrup, manuka honey and coconut sugar, and use them in recipes and baking in place of processed sugars.

✦ **Superfoods, to add to smoothies.** Lucuma, spirulina, maca and chlorella are my favourites.

✦ **Turmeric.** Not only does this add an amazing depth of colour to foods, but it brings with it lots of natural anti-inflammatory properties, too. I love sprinkling it over fried eggs.

✦ **Xanthan gum.** Wonderful for gluten-free cooking.

✦ **Blender**

✦ **Spiraliser.** This handy gadget turns vegetables into long, fine strands that can be eaten in place of pasta, as in my 'courgetti' recipe on page 80.

✦ **Thermometer or Thermapen**

✦ **Seed and nut blitzer (or coffee grinder)**

✦ **Cafetière**, for green tea.

✦ **Digital scales**, for easy, accurate measurements, especially of very small quantities.

✦ **Food processor**

✦ **Garlic slicer**, whilst not completely essential this handy gadget saves time and effort, plus it means your hands don't end up smelling overwhelmingly of garlic. Bonus!

✦ **Juicer**

✦ Good-quality **spring-form cake tins**, to make it even easier to remove your favourite cakes from the tins.

✦ **Heavy-based saucepans.** If possible, it's really worth investing in these as the heat is evenly distributed.

✦ **Steamer.** Steaming retains all the nutrients in vegetables, but if you don't have a steamer, place the vegetables inside a metal colander, pop this on top of a large saucepan or pot, fill the pan with just enough water so that the colander isn't touching it, then bring to a gentle simmer and cover.

Of course, those in the know will have heard that the wonders of coconut oil don't just stay in the kitchen: being 100% natural and with nothing added, it makes for a fabulous beauty product, too. Read on to find out how we can transform your beauty regime as well...

BEAUTY WITH COCONUT OIL

At first, a lot of people can't quite get their heads around the fact that the same oil you cook with can be used on your hair and skin, too. I guess that it probably does sound odd, or at least until you realise that Lucy Bee is 100% coconut oil, with nothing added – totally pure, totally natural.

As a qualified beauty therapist, I am shocked at just how many chemicals we slather on our skin on any given day. Many beauty products are laden with nasties –

ingredients that we've never even have heard of – and yet we're only too happy to put them on our skin. Skin is the body's biggest organ, and so whatever you put on your skin will be absorbed into the body. When you think about this, doesn't it make sense to use something natural?

As I studied for my beauty therapy qualification, I learned so much about physiology and anatomy, sitting neatly alongside nutrition in caring for your body from the outside in. Coconut oil is the perfect link to heal the body naturally. This is why Lucy Bee makes such a fabulous beauty product; it has so many uses that I can't even begin to list them all. However, my favourites are as a:

✦ **Moisturiser:** Rich in vitamin E, coconut oil can nourish and moisturise even the driest of skins. In fact, you only need to use a small amount, and then simply massage into your skin. It can help soften the appearance of fine lines and plump up the skin, and it's even suitable for oily skin types too. What makes coconut oil so great as a moisturiser is that you really don't need to add anything else – it works amazingly well just as it is.

'BEING 100% NATURAL, COCONUT OIL MAKES A FABULOUS BEAUTY PRODUCT.'

✦ **Make-up remover:** This is my all-time favourite beauty use. All you need to do is warm a small amount of oil between your fingertips before massaging over the skin and wiping away with a cotton pad or face cloth. It even removes waterproof mascara and can help to strengthen eyelashes at the same time. What's not to love?

✦ **Cuticle rub:** If I'm cooking and have a little Lucy Bee left over, I use it to rub into my cuticles. It nourishes them, stimulating new nail growth by increasing circulation in the nail bed.

✦ **Deodorant:** I can already sense a few of you are looking a little sceptical, but this really does work. Rub a small amount under your arms and see for yourself.

✦ **Hair conditioner:** At least once a week, I spend a night in and massage Lucy Bee coconut oil into my hair and scalp. I'll then tie my hair up and leave the oil in overnight to condition my hair. You'll need to give it a couple of shampoos to wash it out, but you'll find your locks are softer and shinier than ever before. I've seen a huge difference and try to do this more often. I must admit, I love to straighten and curl my hair, but since using Lucy Bee it's really helped to condition my locks.

✦ **Body scrub:** If you mix Lucy Bee coconut oil with detoxifying Himalayan salt or Epsom salts, it makes the best body scrub ever – the perfect body preparation before your summer holidays or a big event. You can also apply a thin layer of the Lucy Bee 'magic' directly onto your body, making it feel amazing once you get out of the shower.

✦ **Massage oil:** Lucy Bee is a fantastic massage oil, even for delicate newborn skin. If you want to make your massage oil into a holistic treatment, add some essential oils to the coconut oil. The essential oil aroma you choose can vary depending on your mood and whether you prefer a detoxifying or relaxing treatment.

✦ **Oil pulling:** This is an ancient Ayurvedic treatment for ridding the body of toxins and for whitening teeth. Place between a teaspoon and tablespoon of Lucy Bee coconut oil in your mouth and wait for it to melt, then swish it about, just like you would mouthwash, for anywhere between five and 20 minutes. Then spit it out into the bin, rather than the sink, to avoid blocking the drain.

✦ **Toothpaste:** Believe me when I say that your teeth will feel super clean and look whiter after using coconut oil toothpaste.

AND IT DOESN'T STOP THERE...
Just as coconut oil is good for us, it's also good for our pets. We've seen this first hand with our chickens, as well as the pheasants and ducks who turn up most days at the back door, waiting for their fix of Lucy Bee, water and oats. I breakfast most mornings with the ducks, even though I often end up telling them off for fighting over who gets to eat the most oats. Of course, who can blame them when it's covered in Lucy Bee!

Happily, since we love animals, barely a day goes by when we don't hear from one of our followers telling us how their pet has benefited from Lucy Bee too. We've seen photos of Lucy Bee helping every animal from horses and dogs to cats, geckos, and even tortoises.

If that weren't enough, we've even greased garden shears with Lucy Bee, successfully fixed a pair of shoes that wouldn't zip up after one wear (and it's still working fine to this day) and eased a stiff sash window. I told you that Lucy Bee is a versatile and miracle oil!

'COCONUT OIL IS THE PERFECT LINK TO HEAL THE BODY NATURALLY.'

BODY SCRUB

1 tbsp coconut oil
1 tbsp Himalayan salt or Epsom salts
8–12 drops essential oil (choose rose oil for
    calming, eucalyptus for energising or
    lemon for detoxing)
Dry body brush

Place the coconut oil, salts and essential oils
in a ceramic dish and mix until thoroughly
combined. Using a dry body brush, brush the
oil all over your body. Always work the strokes
of the body brush in the direction towards
your heart.

MASSAGE OIL

1 tbsp coconut oil
6–8 drops essential oil or blend (consult a
    practitioner to learn which essential oils
    are best for you)

Place the coconut oil and essential oil or
blend in a ceramic dish and mix until
thoroughly combined.

TOOTHPASTE

1 tbsp coconut oil, slightly softened
1 tbsp bicarbonate of soda
3 drops edible peppermint oil (optional)

Place the coconut oil, bicarbonate of soda and
edible peppermint oil, if using, in a ceramic
dish and mix well together. Use as you would a
normal toothpaste.
    Keep this in a small container in the
bathroom. The first couple of times you use
this toothpaste, you will notice it can taste
different from shop-bought toothpaste, but
stick with it because you will be pleased with
the results. Bicarbonate of soda is softer than
tooth enamel so does not damage your teeth.

BREAKFAST
& BRUNCH

I'm a granola addict and find it difficult to restrain myself from eating this by the handful — it's simply irresistible! Homemade coconut granola is great at any time of the day, not just for breakfast, as it really boosts my energy levels and sends them soaring. For breakfast, I have a bowlful of granola served with my homemade Almond Milk (see page 182), but this also tastes good on top of crumbles, yoghurt or pancakes — go wild!

COCONUT GRANOLA

60g Lucy Bee coconut oil, melted
100g gluten-free oats
50g chia seeds
1 tsp ground ginger
1 tsp ground cinnamon
50g pecan nuts
30g desiccated coconut
50g sultanas
50g big juicy raisins
40g hazelnuts
30g pumpkin seeds

SERVES 4

GF | WF | DF | LF | V

Preheat the oven to 140°C/275°F/gas mark 1. Line a baking tray with baking parchment.

Place all the dry ingredients in a mixing bowl, add the melted coconut oil and stir well using a wooden spoon, until coated in the oil. Tip onto the prepared tray, ensuring that the mixture is spread out evenly.

Bake in the oven for 50 minutes, stirring a couple of times to make sure it doesn't stick and burn. Remove from the oven and leave to cool for 10 minutes. If you want extra-crunchy granola, turn the oven off and leave the door open, with the granola still inside.

VARIATIONS
For extra sweetness, add 1 tsp lucuma powder to the granola mixture. For a chocolate fix, add 30g cacao nibs.

PRE-WORKOUT SCRAMBLED EGG

1 tsp Lucy Bee coconut oil
½ chilli, finely chopped
2 spring onions, finely chopped
2 or 3 medium eggs, beaten
2 large handfuls of spinach, washed
20g feta, crumbled

TO SERVE
½ avocado, chopped
Squeeze of lime juice, to taste

SERVES 1

This amazing breakfast fills me with energy for the day ahead. It's full of good fats to really put a spring in your step – nothing else is required, except maybe a Bulletproof Coffee (see page 43)!

Melt the coconut oil in a non-stick saucepan over a medium heat and add the chilli and spring onions. Gently sauté until softened.

Add the beaten eggs to the pan, then throw in the spinach. Stir until it resembles scrambled egg. Stir in the feta, then spoon onto a plate and serve with the avocado and a squeeze of lime.

SWEET POTATO AND FRIED EGG WITH ROCKET

140g purple sprouting broccoli
2 tsp Lucy Bee coconut oil
Cooked sweet potato, diced
½ tsp dried chilli flakes, or to taste
1 medium egg
Himalayan salt and ground
    black pepper
Handful of rocket, to serve

SERVES 1

This dish is simply the best, especially when you have leftover sweet potato, as it's super-quick, easy and nutritious. Start your day with the right foods to fuel your body, and you'll soon see a difference.

Steam the sprouting broccoli for about 4 minutes, until cooked.

Meanwhile, melt half the coconut oil in a small frying pan over a medium heat. Add the sweet potato and chilli flakes and cook until warmed through. Tip onto a plate.

Melt the remaining coconut oil in the pan, crack the egg into it and fry to your liking, then season. Transfer to the plate along with the steamed broccoli. Add some rocket on the side and serve.

Sometimes — usually the morning after the night before — you need a good fry-up to get you going; these sautéed tomatoes really finish things off a treat. They're the perfect addition to a brunch and are great on a slice of gluten-free toast, topped off with a fried or poached egg. For a fantastically filling and nutritious lunch, serve on a slice of polenta, scattered with chopped parsley or chives. Or add to an omelette with pancetta, samphire and thyme sprigs.

SLOW SAUTÉED TOMATOES

5–10g Lucy Bee coconut oil
400g cherry tomatoes
Pinch of dried thyme
Himalayan salt and ground
   black pepper

SERVES 2

Melt the coconut oil in a heavy-based frying pan over a low heat.

Add the tomatoes and thyme, season well with salt and pepper. (Don't skimp, the seasoning really adds flavour and depth to the tomatoes.) Cover and cook for 20 minutes.

Remove the lid and continue cooking for 10 minutes to reduce the liquid. Dish up alongside a delicious Lucy Bee-style fry up!

For some reason, smoked salmon always feels like a real treat. It reminds me of brunch on Christmas Day, so having this tasty breakfast midweek or at the weekend really fills me with joy. A drizzle of balsamic vinegar over the top works well.

SCRAMBLED EGG WITH SMOKED SALMON AND AVOCADO

1 large avocado, sliced
6 slices of smoked salmon, or to your taste
Lemon juice, to taste
4 medium eggs
2 tsp Lucy Bee coconut oil
1 tbsp chopped parsley
Himalayan salt and ground black pepper

SERVES 2

Arrange half a sliced avocado and three slices of smoked salmon on each plate. Squeeze over lemon juice and sprinkle with salt and pepper to taste.

Crack the eggs into a bowl and season, before lightly beating together.

Melt the coconut oil in a non-stick saucepan over a medium heat, then add the eggs and stir continuously until they thicken to your preferred consistency, making sure you don't overcook them or they will turn dry. As they will continue to cook even after you remove them from the heat, take them off the heat just before you think they are ready.

Spoon the scrambled eggs onto the plates, sprinkle over some parsley and serve immediately.

Breakfast is my favourite meal of the day as it's so important for keeping you healthy and happy, yet so many people seem to skip it. However, there's no excuse to miss breakfast when you can have this filling and nutritious porridge before you head off for the day. Choose your own toppings, as pretty much anything goes.

PORRIDGE OATS, LUCY BEE STYLE

40g gluten-free oats
200ml almond milk, or water
1 tsp Lucy Bee coconut oil

TOPPING SUGGESTIONS

Mix and match toppings, according to your preference:
• ½ banana, sliced • blueberries
• raspberries • strawberries • goji berries • hazelnuts • pumpkin seeds
• toasted hemp seeds • 1 tsp ground cinnamon • 1 tsp nut butter • 1 tsp manuka honey • 1 tsp cacao nibs and/or raw chocolate sauce.
If you like protein powders, you can also add these – I use a vegan protein powder, which I stir into the porridge for an extra boost.

Put the oats, almond milk or water and coconut oil in a saucepan and gently bring to a boil. Once it bubbles and the oats have absorbed the liquid, stir well, remove from the heat and leave to rest for 3–4 minutes.

Pour into a bowl and scatter over your chosen topping or toppings.

SERVES 1

GF   WF   DF   LF   V

These savoury muffins, which are actually more frittatas than muffins, taste lovely when eaten warm, fresh from the oven, and are just as delicious at room temperature. In our house, they barely make it to the table as everyone fights over them. They make an excellent breakfast on-the-go.

SMOKED HADDOCK AND HORSERADISH MUFFINS

275g smoked haddock
50ml milk
15g Lucy Bee coconut oil
100g leeks, rinsed and finely sliced
1 garlic clove, finely chopped
    or crushed
4 large eggs
2 tsp horseradish sauce or
    1 tsp fresh grated horseradish
10g Parmesan, grated
Himalayan salt and ground
    black pepper

SERVES 4 (MAKES 8 MUFFINS)

GF   WF

Preheat the oven to 180°C/350°F/gas mark 4. Line a muffin tin with 8 paper muffin cases. Alternatively, grease 8 moulds of the tin with a little coconut oil.

Place the smoked haddock in a shallow oven dish, pour over the milk, cover the dish with foil and cook in the oven for 15 minutes. Drain and set aside until cool enough to handle.

Meanwhile, heat the coconut oil in a heavy-based frying pan and add the leeks and garlic. Cover and sauté for 5 minutes until softened, then remove the lid and cook off any liquid.

Beat the eggs with some salt, pepper and the horseradish sauce or fresh grated horseradish. Flake the haddock into small pieces and stir into the egg mixture.

Spoon the mixture into the muffin cases or tin, then sprinkle the Parmesan over and bake in the oven for 20–25 minutes. Leave to cool for 5 minutes, before transferring to a wire rack. Serve hot or leave to cool.

This is a good way to start your day, and the ideal breakfast recipe to help you think outside the cereal box. The quinoa will keep you full all morning, and will help those energy levels to soar. I like to serve this with a slice of gluten-free bread to mop up any egg yolk and tomato juices.

QUINOA-STUFFED MUSHROOMS WITH GARLIC TOMATOES AND POACHED EGG

40g quinoa
200ml water or vegetable stock
8 cherry tomatoes, halved
1 garlic clove, finely chopped
1 tbsp Lucy Bee coconut oil, melted
4 flat mushrooms, ideally Portobello,
    stalks removed
Handful of cashew nuts (optional)
2 medium eggs
Handful of baby spinach leaves
Himalayan salt and ground
    black pepper

TO SERVE
Chopped parsley or pea shoots
Slices of gluten-free bread

SERVES 2

GF WF DF LF VEG

Preheat the oven to 180°C/350°F/gas mark 4.

Put the quinoa and water or stock (for more flavour) in a pan and cook over a medium heat for 10–12 minutes, until softened. Drain and set aside.

Place the tomato halves on a baking tray, sprinkle with the garlic, drizzle over half the coconut oil, and season with salt and pepper. Place the mushrooms and cashew nuts, if using, on a separate baking tray and brush with the remaining coconut oil, then place both trays in the oven and bake the tomatoes for 15 minutes and the mushrooms and cashew nuts for 10 minutes.

Stuff the cooked mushrooms with the drained quinoa, then return to the oven for a further 5 minutes.

Meanwhile, add boiling water to about a 10cm depth to a saucepan. Lower the heat so that the water is just off the boil, then crack both eggs into the water and cook for 3 minutes (for a runny yolk). Remove with a slotted spoon.

Spread a layer of spinach across each plate, then add the mushrooms and cashew nuts. Scatter the tomatoes over the mushrooms and then place poached egg on top. Season, scatter over chopped parsley or pea shoots, then serve immediately with slices of gluten-free bread.

As my followers on social media will know, I have a slight addiction to pancakes, but thankfully my addiction is a healthy one. There are SO many different ways to make pancakes. I like using either quinoa flakes, buckwheat flour (despite the name this is actually a fruit seed and is gluten-free) or oats.

PANCAKES ANYONE?

1 banana
2 eggs
40g quinoa flakes
1 tsp ground cinnamon
1 tsp Lucy Bee coconut oil

TOPPING SUGGESTIONS

- Walnuts and pumpkin seeds with cinnamon and manuka honey
- Greek yoghurt with fruit
- Banana, peanut butter and cacao nibs
- Salted Chocolate Almond Butter (see page 182)
- Almond milk, cacao and manuka honey (blended together to make a sauce) with berries
- Lemon juice with coconut sugar
- Greek yoghurt with Healthy Seed Mix (see page 182)

SERVES 1

Put the bananas, eggs, quinoa flakes and cinnamon in a blender and blend together.

Melt the coconut oil in a small frying pan, then pour in the pancake mixture in batches to make small pancakes. Fry for 3 minutes on each side until cooked through.

Serve with a selection of toppings, either from the list of suggestions (see left) or your own favourite – the world's your oyster!

BREAKFAST & BRUNCH

OVERNIGHT CHIA AND COCONUT PUDDING WITH SAUTÉED BANANA

50g chia seeds
30g coconut yoghurt
200ml almond milk
½ tsp ground cinnamon
½ tsp ground nutmeg
1 tbsp desiccated coconut (optional)
1 tsp manuka honey
1 banana
1 tbsp Lucy Bee coconut oil
1 tbsp pomegranate seeds

**SERVES 2 GENEROUSLY,
OR 4 SMALL SERVINGS**

GF WF DF LF VEG

So many people fall back on cereals for breakfast, but they're usually laden with sugar and won't keep you full or happy until lunchtime. This is a great alternative breakfast option that will pack your body with healthy fuel for the day ahead. Sleep is a time machine to breakfast – I often go to sleep dreaming of this after making it for the following morning.

Put the chia seeds, coconut yoghurt and almond milk into a small bowl. Stir in the cinnamon, nutmeg, desiccated coconut, if using, and honey, then pour into two (or four) bowls or glasses and leave to set in the fridge overnight.

When ready to serve, slice the banana about 2cm thick. Sauté in a frying pan with coconut oil over a high heat for 1–2 minutes or until caramelised.

Spoon banana slices on top of each chilled pudding and then scatter over a handful pomegranate seeds.

VARIATION

Instead of banana, sauté chopped apple in coconut oil that has been infused with cloves: Heat the oil gently in a pan and add 4 cloves. After a couple of minutes the clove aroma will be released. Remove the cloves from the pan and add the chopped apple to sauté.

BREAKFAST BANANA AND KIWI WITH TOFU AND CHIA SEEDS

20g Lucy Bee coconut oil
100g ripe banana
175g kiwi, peeled
200g silken tofu
40g chia seeds
50g cashew nuts

SERVES 2–3

GF WF DF LF V

While this may sound like an odd combination, trust me when I say that it tastes phenomenal. The silken tofu is incredibly creamy, which will make this dish feel as though you're eating dessert for breakfast – and that's never a bad way to start the day, right?

Blend all the ingredients together in a food processor until smooth. Leave to stand for 30 minutes to thicken, then serve in bowls.

GREEN TOFU SMOOTHIE

20g Lucy Bee coconut oil
200ml coconut water
100g silken tofu
30g spinach, ½ avocado, 1 kiwi, peeled
    and 50g mango or pineapple flesh
1 tsp lucuma powder
1 tbsp Healthy Seed Mix (see page 182)

When you're running low on time in the morning, this makes a great breakfast on-the-go. Simply blitz it up, pour it into a recycled Lucy Bee jar, and run!

Put all the ingredients in a blender, then blitz to a smooth mixture. Serve immediately, topped with desiccated coconut, goji berries or cacao nibs if you like.

SERVES 1

MANGO LASSI

1 tsp Lucy Bee coconut oil
Flesh of 1 mango
100ml kefir (or natural yoghurt)
50ml almond milk
1 tsp orange blossom water
1 tsp manuka honey
Seeds of 1 cardamom pod, crushed

Kefir is a cultured milk that is rich in healthy probiotic bacteria, as well as being a good source of B vitamins, minerals and essential amino acids.

Put all the ingredients in a blender and blitz together until smooth and thick. Serve immediately.

SERVES 1

BLUEBERRY BEE BLITZ

1 tsp Lucy Bee coconut oil
50g frozen blueberries
1 small or ½ medium banana
100ml kefir (or natural yoghurt)
50ml coconut milk

This smoothie works brilliantly made with frozen blueberries, so always keep your freezer stocked.

Put all the ingredients in a blender and blitz together until smooth and thick. Serve immediately.

SERVES 1

BULLETPROOF COFFEE

15–20g Lucy Bee coconut oil
1 shot of espresso coffee
15–20g grass-fed, organic,
    unsalted butter

This is the ultimate pre-workout drink. Plus, it tastes every bit as creamy as your favourite latte.

Put all the ingredients into a blender and blend until completely combined. This ensures the oil doesn't separate and lie on the top.

SERVES 1

LUNCH BITES

Sushi is actually incredibly easy to make and is a really tasty and nutritious lunch or supper. I find that sushi fillings tend to be a really personal thing, so mix and match according to your mood, and it's a great recipe to make with friends so that you can all try out your favourites.

BROWN RICE OR QUINOA SUSHI

170g brown rice or quinoa
225ml water
1 tbsp Lucy Bee coconut oil
Dash of rice vinegar
4–6 nori sheets

FILLING SUGGESTIONS
- Avocado, sliced
- Smoked salmon, shredded
- Cream cheese
- Red pepper, finely sliced
- Cucumber, peeled, deseeded and cut into matchsticks

SERVES 2–4

GF | WF

Place the rice or quinoa in a saucepan. Add the water and the coconut oil, with the rice vinegar if using. Over a low heat, gently simmer the rice or quinoa until cooked, adding a little more water if necessary to prevent it from burning. Alternatively, cook the rice or quinoa according to the packet instructions. Once cooked, set the rice or quinoa aside to cool.

Lay a nori sheet on a lined tray, rough side up. Spread a thin layer of cooked, cooled rice or quinoa evenly over the sheet, leaving a 2.5cm border on the side furthest away from you. Scatter over your choice of filling, without overcrowding them.

Pick up the side of the nori sheet closest to you and gently start to roll the sheet, keeping it nice and tight. When you get to the side furthest from you, wet it with your finger to ensure that the nori sticks together. Repeat with the remaining nori sheets, rice and fillings.

Wet a very sharp knife and cut the rolled sushi into roughly 2.5cm sushi bites, keeping the knife wet in between each cut, and avoiding touching the nori too much with your hands. Each nori sheet will make between 6–8 sushi bites.

Serve the sushi on plates with a bowl of soy sauce for dipping as the perfect finger food.

Exotic mushrooms with hard-to-pronounce names are now being grown in the UK, which is good news as they are not only delicious but come with many health benefits too. Varieties such as enoki, shiitake, oyster and shimeji are becoming more widely available, and are immune-boosting wonders.

CREAMY SAGE POLENTA WITH EXOTIC MUSHROOMS

FOR THE POLENTA
500ml milk or almond milk
200ml water
1 sage sprig (about 6 leaves), plus
   extra fried in a little coconut oil
   until crisp, to serve (optional)
75g instant polenta
1 tsp flaky sea salt
1 tbsp Lucy Bee coconut oil, melted
15g Parmesan, grated

FOR THE MUSHROOMS
1 tbsp Lucy Bee coconut oil
150g mixed exotic mushrooms
Dash of fish sauce
80g broccoli, cut into small florets
   and steamed
Himalayan salt and ground black
   pepper

SERVES 2

GF   WF

Put the milk, water and sage into a saucepan and bring almost to the boil. Pour in the polenta and salt, whisking as you go, and continue to whisk over a low heat until the polenta is a porridge-like consistency, 5–7 minutes.

Stir in the melted coconut oil and remove from the heat. Remove the sage and add the Parmesan, stirring with a wooden spoon.

For the mushrooms, heat the coconut oil in large frying pan and add the mushrooms. Sauté for a couple of minutes, adding the fish sauce, until tender. Stir in the steamed broccoli florets and season to taste.

Serve the creamy polenta in shallow bowls with the mushrooms on top, garnished with crispy fried sage leaves, if using.

When I was younger, one of the things I felt I missed out on was chicken nuggets. My Uncle Ash used to make these healthy, gluten-free chicken fingers all the time and they were so tasty that my friends only ever wanted his version of nuggets. Eventually, they became known as AFC (Ash's Favourite Chicken)! These are ideal to serve to friends with dips, with Celeriac Fries (see page 116) or Roasted Sweet Potato Wedges (see page 120) or with a green salad.

CHICKEN FINGERS

3 tsp mild curry powder (or see page 181 for homemade)
1 tsp five-spice powder
1 tsp dried tarragon
Pinch of celery salt (optional)
Pinch of sweet paprika (optional)
400g skinless chicken fillets or chicken breast cut into finger-sized pieces
2 medium eggs, beaten
200g gluten-free breadcrumbs
50g Lucy Bee coconut oil

SERVES 2–4

GF   WF   LF   DF

In a medium-large bowl, mix together the curry powder, five-spice and tarragon, with the celery salt and paprika if using, then add the chicken pieces and turn to coat in the mixture. Leave to stand for 10–20 minutes.

Put the beaten eggs and breadcrumbs into two separate shallow dishes. Dip each chicken piece first in the egg, then coat in the breadcrumbs and place on a plate.

Heat the coconut oil in a heavy-based frying pan until hot, then add the chicken and cook for about 4 minutes before turning and cooking for a further 4 minutes, depending on thickness. If unsure, check they are cooked using a Thermapen (thermometer).

Sometimes, all you want to do is kick back on the sofa and cosy up in front of the TV with your favourite comfort food. However, this pizza will change your life. I mean, what's not to love about turning something bad on its head and making it completely healthy and gluten-free? These are my favourite toppings, but feel free to play around with your own combinations.

CAULIFLOWER PIZZA

FOR THE BASE

1 medium cauliflower,
   roughly chopped
2 eggs, lightly beaten
20g buckwheat flour
2 tsp mixed dried herbs
Pinch of Dukkah Spiced Seed Mix
   (see page 181) or dried chilli flakes
1 tbsp Lucy Bee coconut oil, melted
Himalayan salt and ground
   black pepper

FOR THE TOMATO SAUCE

1 tbsp Lucy Bee coconut oil
3 large garlic cloves, crushed
1 x 400g tin chopped tomatoes
Juice of ½ lemon
1 tsp mixed dried herbs or 3 fresh
   thyme sprigs (optional)

TOPPING SUGGESTIONS

- Buffalo mozzarella and fresh basil
- Goat's cheese and watercress
- Kalamata olives and crumbled feta
- Smoked salmon and rocket
   (add just before serving)

SERVES 4

Preheat the oven to 180°C/350°F/gas mark 4. Line a flat baking tray (a non-stick pizza baking tray is ideal) with baking parchment.

Blitz the cauliflower in a food processor until it resembles rice grains. Transfer to a bowl and stir in the beaten eggs, buckwheat flour, herbs, spiced seed mix or chilli flakes, and some seasoning. Knead the mixture to a dough-like consistency.

Roll out the dough evenly and thinly on the lined tray, making either one or two bases. A good technique is to spread out the dough, place cling film over the top and, using a rolling pin, roll out. Using a pastry brush, brush the melted coconut oil over each base. Bake in the oven for 25–30 minutes, until crispy.

Meanwhile, to make the tomato sauce, melt the coconut oil in a saucepan, add the garlic and sauté until golden, then add the chopped tomatoes, lemon juice and herbs. Simmer for 20 minutes uncovered until the sauce almost resembles a paste, taking care as the sauce may stick to the pan.

Spread the tomato sauce over the cooked bases and add your choice of toppings. If the toppings need cooking, cook in the oven for a further 15 minutes.

PEPPERS AND TOMATOES WITH ANCHOVIES ON POLENTA

1 tbsp Lucy Bee coconut oil, plus extra for frying
1 x 50g tin anchovies in oil
2 garlic cloves, thinly sliced
600g peppers, a mixture of colours, deseeded and thinly sliced
200g cherry tomatoes
Cooked polenta, cut into pieces 5 x 3cm (large fudge size)
Handful of torn basil or rocket leaves, to serve

SERVES 2

I love this Mediterranean-style combination of flavours. Close your eyes and you could almost be lunching in Italy. Any leftovers taste great the next day, on their own or in an omelette.

Put the coconut oil, anchovies and garlic in a heavy-based frying pan over a medium heat. Add the peppers and tomatoes, give it a good stir, then cook over a medium heat for 15 minutes, until the peppers have softened. Tip into a bowl and keep warm.

Add a touch more coconut oil to the wiped-out pan and, when hot, add the polenta pieces and fry on each side until golden.

Place the polenta on a plate, spoon the pepper mixture over and serve topped with basil or rocket leaves.

POLENTA WITH CHILLI

1 litre water
250g instant polenta
2 tsp Himalayan salt
2 tsp ground black pepper
Few shakes of dried chilli flakes
1 tbsp Lucy Bee coconut oil

SERVES 6–8

This spiced polenta makes a lovely side dish or addition to salads or roasted vegetables. If you like having something starchy to mop up your dinner, this spiced polenta makes an excellent alternative to sweet or roast potatoes. Delicious!

Place the water in a large saucepan and bring to the boil. Turn the heat down to low and tip in the polenta in a steady stream, stirring constantly. Continue stirring as the polenta thickens, about 3 minutes.

Stir in the salt, pepper, chilli flakes and coconut oil. Pour the polenta into a square or rectangular dish and leave to set – when ready, it should be firm to the touch.

When ready to serve, tip the polenta out of the dish and cut into pieces, as required. It will keep for a few days in the fridge and also freezes well.

VARIATION
For a cheesy version, stir in 50g grated Parmesan along with the seasonings.

This is my ultimate mid-week meal as it's packed full of flavour and goodness. Sometimes it's easy to get a little stuck with lunch ideas, and this is also a great dish to make in bulk and take to work in a lunchbox the next day. Kelp noodles are popular in Asian cooking and work brilliantly with fragrant or spicy dishes. They're also a nutritional powerhouse, so dish up and dose up on your vitamins and minerals!

MARINATED TOFU STIR-FRY WITH KELP NOODLES AND ASIAN GREENS

200g firm tofu, cut into 2cm cubes
200g kelp noodles or rice noodles
30g Lucy Bee coconut oil
8 spring onions, cut into matchsticks
1 red pepper, deseeded and sliced
1 green pepper, deseeded and sliced
1 pak choi or tat soi, or a mixture, chopped
Ground black pepper
Alfalfa sprouts, to serve

FOR THE MARINADE
2 garlic cloves, crushed
30g fresh ginger, peeled and chopped
10g fresh horseradish, peeled and chopped
4 tsp sesame oil
6 tsp tamari
40ml rice wine vinegar

SERVES 2–4

GF | WF | DF | LF | V

Blitz the marinade ingredients together in a food processor, then transfer to a bowl. Add the cubed tofu to the marinade, stir to coat, then set aside to marinate for at least 2 hours.

Cook the kelp or rice noodles according to the packet instructions. Once cooked, set the noodles aside. Heat the coconut oil in a wok or heavy-based frying pan, then add the tofu along with the marinade and cook for 2 minutes, stirring occasionally. Add the spring onions, peppers and pak choi or tat soi, and cook for 3 minutes.

Meanwhile, submerge the noodles in cold water for 1 minute, then drain and stir into the tofu and vegetables, mixing until the noodles are coated in the sauce. Add black pepper to taste and serve with a scattering of alfalfa sprouts.

People are always asking me for lunch ideas, or alternatives to sandwiches and salads, and these fritters are one of my favourites to pack into lunchboxes as a light bite. They work equally well as a side dish or as finger food for relaxed lunches with friends. I serve these fritters with a refreshing tzatziki.

CARROT, SWEET POTATO AND FETA FRITTERS WITH TZATZIKI

3 large carrots, peeled and grated
1 sweet potato, peeled and grated
1 red onion, peeled and grated
1 garlic clove, crushed
1 heaped tsp ras el hanout (optional)
3 medium eggs, beaten
3 tbsp chickpea flour or other
    gluten-free flour
100g feta, crumbled
Handful of fresh parsley leaves,
    chopped
1 tbsp Lucy Bee coconut oil
Himalayan salt and ground
    black pepper

FOR THE TZATZIKI

1 garlic clove
½ cucumber, peeled and deseeded
100g Greek yoghurt
Handfull of chopped fresh mint
    (optional)
Himalayan salt and ground
    black pepper

SERVES 4

To make the tzatziki, place the garlic with 1 tsp of salt in a pestle and mortar. Blend to a very fine paste. Grate the peeled cucumber into a clean tea towel, then squeeze to remove as much liquid as possible. Place the cucumber into a bowl, then add the remaining ingredients and combine thoroughly. Place in the fridge until ready to serve.

In a large mixing bowl, mix the grated carrots, sweet potato and red onion, then mix in the garlic and ras el hanout, if using.

In a separate bowl, whisk together the beaten eggs and flour, then stir into the vegetables with the feta and parsley.

Melt the coconut oil in a frying pan over a medium heat. Shape the fritter ingredients into patty-sized balls, then, working in batches, add to the frying pan and flatten using a spatula.

Cook for about 3 minutes each side, being careful not to burn them. Serve golden and slightly crunchy with a dollop of Tzatziki.

FALAFEL BITES

GF WF DF LF V

1 x 400g tin chickpeas, drained
   and rinsed
20g Lucy Bee coconut oil, plus extra
   for frying
2 garlic cloves, crushed
1 tbsp ground cumin
½ tsp ground coriander
Pinch of dried chilli flakes
Grated zest of ½ lime
½ tsp bicarbonate of soda
2 spring onions, finely chopped
5 tbsp fresh coriander leaves,
   chopped
Himalayan salt and ground
   black pepper

SERVES 4

When I was little, I used to eat these moreish bites with Indian take-aways or homemade curries, in place of onion bhajis. Now, I like to add them to gluten-free wraps for a nutritious and filling lunch, or I'll just grab them and eat them on-the-go.

Blitz together all the ingredients in a food processor, then tip the mixture into a bowl and place in the fridge to firm up, about 30 minutes.

Using dessert spoonfuls of mixture, form into flat, round cakes. Place on a baking tray and refrigerate for 30 minutes.

Heat 3–4 tbsp coconut oil in a large, non-stick frying pan and cook the falafels for about 5 minutes, turning occasionally, until crisp and brown. Lift out with a slotted spoon and drain on kitchen paper.

Serve with Gluten-free Flatbreads (see page 183), Sun-dried Tomato Hummus (see page 178) and Tabbouleh with Tahini Dressing (see below).

TABBOULEH WITH TAHINI DRESSING

GF WF DF LF V

125g buckwheat
180ml water
20g Lucy Bee coconut oil, melted
150g ripe tomatoes, chopped
2 spring onions, finely sliced
Juice of 1 lime
1 tsp Baharat spice mix (see page 181)
80g flat-leaf parsley sprigs, leaves only
20g mint sprigs, leaves only
Himalayan salt and ground
   black pepper

FOR THE TAHINI DRESSING
1 garlic clove, crushed
2 tbsp tahini, stirred well
1 tbsp Lucy Bee coconut oil, melted
Juice of 1 lime
Pinch of Himalayan salt

SERVES 4

Traditionally tabbouleh is made with bulgar, or cracked wheat, but fortunately there are some wonderful wheat- and gluten-free 'grains' (which are really seeds), such as quinoa and buckwheat than can be used as substitutes.

Place the buckwheat in a saucepan. Add the 180ml water and the coconut oil. Bring to the boil, cover, and then leave to cook on a low heat for 12–15 minutes. Alternatively, cook the buckwheat according to the packet instructions. Once cooked, set the buckwheat aside to cool and transfer to a serving bowl. Add the tomatoes and spring onions along with the lime juice and spice mix.

Slice the parsley and mint leaves as finely as possible, using a slicing motion rather than chopping down onto the board, to prevent the flavour seeping out. Add the herbs to the serving bowl and mix. Season to taste.

Blend together all the ingredients for the tahini dressing and serve with the tabbouleh.

This is a wonderful pâté, so simple to make and perfect for serving on gluten-free bread, jacket potatoes, or even stirred into soups. A traditional pâté uses butter, which we've substituted with coconut oil so it is great for those who are lactose intolerant. We enjoy this pâté on special occasions, such as a starter on Christmas Day, and is my Auntie Judy and Uncle Ron's favourite.

CHICKEN LIVER PÂTÉ

200g Lucy Bee coconut oil,
    plus extra to finish
400g organic chicken livers, cut in
    half and any sinew trimmed off
6 shallots, finely chopped
2 garlic cloves, chopped
2 tsp fresh thyme leaves
1 tsp ground allspice
Himalayan salt and ground
    black pepper

TO SERVE
Gluten-free bread, toasted
Gherkins and small pickles
Lemon wedges

SERVES 8

| GF | WF | DF | LF |

Melt 50g of the coconut oil in a large frying pan. Add the chicken livers and cook over a medium heat for 4–6 minutes, turning during cooking. Do not overcook, the livers should still be pink on the inside. Remove from the pan using a slotted spoon and set aside.

Melt another 50g coconut oil in the pan, add the shallots and fry over a medium heat, adding a touch more oil if required, until softened; do not let them colour.

Stir through the garlic, half the thyme leaves and the allspice, and cook for 2 minutes. Remove from the heat and add the remaining coconut oil, stirring until melted and combined.

Tip the livers and the shallot mixture into a food processor, with salt and pepper to taste. Process until smooth, then taste and adjust the seasoning if necessary.

Using a spatula, scrape the mixture into a pretty serving bowl, smoothing over the surface. Place in the fridge to set for about 1 hour.

Brush the surface of the set pâté with a little more coconut oil and scatter over the remaining thyme leaves. Serve with toasted gluten-free bread, gherkins, pickles and lemon wedges.

This pâté will keep, covered, in the fridge for a few days, but I recommend you remove it to room temperature about an hour before eating.

GOAT'S CHEESE AND ROCKET FRITTATA

1 tbsp Lucy Bee coconut oil
2 red onions, thinly sliced
2 large garlic cloves, crushed
200g rocket
2 tbsp chopped parsley
2 tbsp Sun-dried Tomato Pesto
   (see page 178)
6 medium eggs, lightly beaten
75g soft goat's cheese
3 tbsp freshly grated Parmesan
Himalayan salt and ground
   black pepper

SERVES 4

There's something about the classic combination of goat's cheese and rocket that I never grow bored of – it just works. This frittata is great for a cheap and fast evening meal but makes a healthy and filling lunch, too. For an added kick, serve with my Raspberry Chipotle Sauce (see page 176).

Preheat the grill on a medium setting. Melt half of coconut oil in a heavy-based pan, add the onions and sauté over a medium heat until soft. Add the garlic and cook for a further 2 minutes, then tip into a mixing bowl, add the rocket, parsley and pesto, mix together, then add the eggs.

Melt the remaining coconut oil in the frying pan until hot, then pour the mixture into the pan and cook for 2–3 minutes, or until the mixture just starts to set. Scatter the goat's cheese and Parmesan over the top and cook for a further 2 minutes.

Place the pan under the grill for 3–5 minutes, or until the top is golden and bubbling. Leave to stand for 5 minutes before cutting into wedges and serving.

SWEET POTATO AND CHILLI FRITTATA WITH FETA

1 sweet potato, peeled and diced
1 tbsp Lucy Bee coconut oil
1 green chilli, deseeded and sliced
4 medium eggs, beaten
Small handful of fresh coriander
   leaves, chopped
50g feta
Himalayan salt and ground
   black pepper
Rocket, to serve

SERVES 4

When I was working as a beauty therapist full-time, I would often make a frittata the night before, ready to enjoy the next day whilst at work. It lasts well and tastes just as good cold as hot, making it perfect for your lunchbox.

Steam the sweet potato over a pan of boiling water for 10–15 minutes, or until softened.

Preheat the grill on a medium setting. Melt the coconut oil in a frying pan over a medium heat, add the sweet potato and chilli and sauté for 3–4 minutes.

Mix the eggs and coriander together in a jug, then pour over the sweet potato and chilli, before crumbling over the feta. Cook for 2–3 minutes, or until the base is just starting to set, then place the pan under the grill until the top is cooked. Leave to stand for 5 minutes before cutting into wedges and serving with a handful of rocket.

I love omelettes and I couldn't choose just one to share with you, so instead I decided to give you three. Have a go at mixing and matching ingredients to make this basic recipe all the more interesting. Serve with a green salad.

WE'RE TALKING OMELETTES! THREE RECIPES IN ONE

1 tsp Lucy Bee coconut oil
3 medium eggs, beaten
Himalayan salt and ground
   black pepper

SALMON AND SAMPHIRE

20g feta, crumbled
Pinch of dried chilli flakes
Handful of samphire
Smoked salmon, to taste

ROASTED VEGETABLE AND GOAT'S CHEESE

1 tbsp roasted vegetables
1 tbsp cooked sweet potatoes
1 jalapeño chilli, deseeded and sliced
20g goat's cheese
Small handful of parsley, chopped

MY ITALIAN OMELETTE

1 small onion, sliced
1 tomato, sliced
Basil leaves
Mozzarella, torn into pieces
1 tsp dried oregano

SERVES 1

SALMON AND SAMPHIRE

Melt the coconut oil in a frying pan, then add the eggs and season to taste. Sprinkle over the feta and chilli flakes and gently cook for a couple of minutes. Flip the omelette over and cook the other side. Add the samphire and smoked salmon. Fold the omelette in half before serving immediately.

ROASTED VEGETABLE AND GOAT'S CHEESE

Melt the coconut oil in a frying pan and add the roasted vegetables and cooked sweet potato. Sauté until lightly browned, then add the eggs along with the remaining ingredients, before seasoning and cooking on each side.

MY ITALIAN OMELETTE

Melt the coconut oil in a frying pan and sauté the onion and tomato until softened. Add the eggs, basil, mozzarella and oregano, before seasoning and cooking on each side.

QUICK
SUPPERS

This dish is quick to whip up after a long day at work, and tastes amazing – I love the combination of flavours, from the salty olives to the sweetness of the sun-dried tomatoes. Feel free to use different nuts, such as hazelnuts, in the stuffing, which works equally well with fish as with chicken. If you have any of the stuffing mixture left over, it will keep for up to one week when kept in the fridge.

CHICKEN BREAST WITH OLIVE, SAGE AND WALNUTS

4 boneless and skinless
   chicken breasts
100g black Kalamata pitted olives
1 garlic clove, crushed
Handful of fresh sage leaves
75g walnuts or pecans
10g Lucy Bee coconut oil, plus a little
   extra, melted, to drizzle
70g sun-dried tomatoes

FOR THE TOPPING
2 slices of gluten-free bread
Handful of parsley leaves
20g Parmesan

SERVES 4

GF   WF

Preheat the oven to 180°C/350°F/gas mark 4. Line a baking tray with baking parchment.

Cut a slit along the side of each chicken breast to form a pocket. Blitz the remaining ingredients together in a food processor, then stuff into the chicken pockets and transfer to the lined tray.

To make the topping, blitz the ingredients together in a food processor. Sprinkle over the chicken breasts, drizzle with a little melted coconut oil, then cook in the oven for 20–25 minutes, until cooked through (see below).

Serve with Roasted Sweet Potato Wedges (see page 120) and seasonal vegetables.

TIP One of my most used kitchen gadgets is a good meat thermometer, which means you can wave good-bye to dry, over-cooked chicken. It also works a treat if you worry about under-cooking, too. Chicken is cooked when the centre of the thickest piece reaches 74°C/165°F. It is best to cook meat from room temperature rather than straight from the fridge, but don't let it sit out for too long – 15–20 minutes will do.

CHICKEN MASALA SKEWERS

4 boneless, skinless chicken breasts, cubed or cut into bite-size pieces

FOR THE MARINADE
½ tsp cumin seeds
½ tsp coriander seeds
½ tsp grated lime zest
½ tsp dried mint
1 tbsp Lucy Bee coconut oil, melted
Juice of 1 lime
100g Greek yoghurt
Thumb-sized piece of fresh ginger, peeled and finely grated
1 garlic clove, peeled and crushed
1 fresh green chilli, deseeded and finely sliced
1 green pepper, finely chopped
Himalayan salt and ground black pepper

TO SERVE
Handful of coriander leaves, chopped
Handful of mint leaves, chopped
Lime wedges

SERVES 4

For all you fans of Indian food and take-aways, these fantastic skewers are a healthy option and are great on the barbecue, or as a finger food served with my Carrot, Sweet Potato and Feta Fritters (see page 57), or with my Fruity Mango Salsa (see page 182) and a salad with Lemon Garlic Dressing (see page 175).

Preheat the oven to 120°C/250°F/gas ½.

Spread the cumin and coriander seeds and the lime zest out on a baking tray and toast in the oven for about 10 minutes. Grind to a coarse powder using a pestle and mortar. Add the ground spices to the remaining marinade ingredients in a large mixing bowl, then season well and stir. Add the chicken pieces. Cover and refrigerate overnight, for the chicken to marinate.

When ready to cook, preheat the overhead grill to hot or light the barbecue and waiting until it is at a high heat. Thread the chicken pieces onto four metal skewers. Grill or barbecue for 8–10 minutes, turning regularly. The chicken may seem to brown quite quickly, but don't be tempted to turn the skewers too soon, as you want it to caramelise them and release all those wonderful flavours.

Serve the chicken skewers immediately with the fresh herbs and lime wedges.

CHICKEN SATAY

4 boneless, skinless chicken breasts, cubed or cut into bite-size pieces

FOR THE SATAY
200ml coconut milk
6 tbsp natural peanut butter
Thumb-sized piece of fresh ginger, peeled and grated (optional, but adds a little spice)
1 tbsp tahini
1 tbsp gluten-free soy sauce
1 tsp dried chilli flakes
10g Lucy Bee coconut oil, plus extra for frying
Juice of 1 lime
1 garlic clove, peeled

SERVES 4–6

With its amazing flavours, this is an absolute favourite with Willis and I. The take-away versions tend to be loaded with hidden nasties and sugars, so I made it my mission to turn this delicious dish into a nutritious meal.

Put the satay ingredients into a blender and process until smooth, then transfer to a bowl.

Melt a little coconut oil in a frying pan over a high heat. Dunk each chicken cube into the sauce, before adding to the frying pan. Fry for 8–10 minutes, turning frequently, until cooked through. Once cooked, serve with brown rice and fresh vegetables.

VARIATIONS
Instead of dunking the chicken cubes in the satay before frying, you can serve the satay alongside as a dipping sauce. For a barbecue, thread the chicken cubes onto skewers and cook for 8–10 minutes over a high heat.

Ginger, lemongrass and chilli go so well together, and the smell you get when cooking these in Lucy Bee coconut oil is truly mouth-watering.

CHICKEN WITH LEMONGRASS, LIME AND CORIANDER

1 tbsp Lucy Bee coconut oil
Thumb-sized piece of fresh ginger, peeled and grated
2 lemongrass stalks, thinly sliced
1 red chilli, deseeded and chopped
6 kaffir lime leaves
400ml coconut milk
2 tsp sugar (palm, coconut or any natural alternative)
4 boneless, skinless chicken thighs
1 tbsp lime juice
Handful of coriander leaves, roughly chopped, to serve

Melt the coconut oil in a frying pan, then add the ginger, lemongrass and chilli and gently sauté.

Stir in the lime leaves, coconut milk and sugar, then bring to a gentle simmer and cook, uncovered, at a relaxed bubble for around 5 minutes.

Add the chicken, then cover and simmer for about 25 minutes, until tender and cooked. Stir in the lime juice and scatter the coriander over before serving with brown rice and steamed broccoli.

SERVES 4

GF   WF   DF   LF

This dish combines two of my favourite ingredients — chicken and chorizo — and is the perfect meal to eat al fresco, while pretending you're holidaying in the Mediterranean. It also tastes just as good the next day eaten cold, as the flavours are enhanced.

CHICKEN AND CHORIZO PAELLA

40g Lucy Bee coconut oil
1 onion, finely chopped
½ cooking chorizo, chopped
4 garlic cloves, crushed
400g risotto or paella rice
1 level tsp smoked paprika
   (sweet or hot)
200g roasted red peppers from
   a jar, diced
300g boneless, skinless chicken
   breasts, cut into bite-sized pieces
500ml chicken stock
500ml water
Large pinch of saffron threads
150g cooked broad beans, skins
   removed (frozen are fine)
12 black olives (optional)
Handful of parsley leaves
Himalayan salt and ground
   black pepper
Lemons wedges, to serve

SERVES 4

GF   WF

Melt the coconut oil in a large, heavy-based pan and gently fry the onion and chorizo, until the onion has softened. Add the garlic and sauté for another minute.

Tip in the rice, stir, and cook for 1 minute. Add the smoked paprika, red pepper and chicken and stir it all together.

Pour in the stock, water, saffron, broad beans and olives, if using, then season to taste. Reduce the heat to low, cover and cook for 12–15 minutes, stirring occasionally to prevent sticking. Add the parsley, leave to stand for a few minutes and serve with lemon wedges, and a green salad.

PAN-FRIED MARINATED SALMON WITH WILTED BABY SPINACH

FOR THE MARINADE
Thumb-sized piece of ginger, peeled
1 garlic clove, peeled
20ml tamari sauce
Juice of 1 lime

2 salmon fillets
20g Lucy Bee coconut oil
80g baby spinach leaves

SERVES 2

Salmon is not only incredibly good for your body, skin and hair, but it's also really quick to prepare. This simple marinade really lifts the salmon fillets too, taking them from delicious to out of this world.

Blitz together the ginger, garlic, tamari and lime juice in a food processor. Place the salmon fillets in a bowl, cover with the mixture and leave to marinate for 30 minutes.

Melt the coconut oil in a heavy-based frying pan, then add the salmon skin side down, along with the marinade, and fry for about 8 minutes, turning halfway through.

Remove to serving plates and keep warm. Add the spinach to the pan and cook until wilted, 3–4 minutes. Add the spinach to the plates alongside the salmon and serve with either rice or quinoa and cherry tomatoes.

VARIATION
For an alternative marinade, use 1 tsp sumac, 1 tsp toasted fennel seeds and the zest and juice of 1 lime.

SALMON WITH PESTO TOPPING

Lucy Bee coconut oil, for greasing
100g Sun-dried Tomato Pesto
   (see page 178), or shop-bought
50g gluten-free breadcrumbs
2 salmon fillets

SERVES 2

This looks like a really impressive dish, but it's surprisingly quick to make. It's packed full of the most wonderful flavours and makes the perfect light lunch or supper to enjoy al fresco in the summer.

Preheat the oven to 180°C/350°F/gas mark 4. Lightly grease a baking tray using a little coconut oil. Mix together the pesto and breadcrumbs.

Place the salmon fillets skin side down on the baking tray and spread the pesto mixture evenly on top. Cook in the oven for 20 minutes or until the salmon is just cooked through.

Serve at once with Sweet Potato Mash with Chives (see page 119) and broccoli or asparagus, or with new potatoes lightly crushed with nori flakes and drizzled with coconut oil, and sautéed samphire.

FISH FINGERS

3 slices of gluten-free bread
1 garlic clove, peeled
50g Parmesan
20g parsley
60g gluten-free flour, seasoned
1 egg, beaten
350g cod loin, cut into finger-
   sized pieces
50g Lucy Bee coconut oil
Himalayan salt and ground
   black pepper
Lemon wedges, to serve

SERVES 2

These delicious, golden fish fingers are another
wonderful unhealthy-to-healthy recipe – your friends
won't complain if you dish these up for supper!

Put the bread, garlic, Parmesan and parsley in a food
processor and blitz until it resembles fine breadcrumbs.
Tip into a dish, and then place the seasoned flour in a
separate dish. Pour the beaten egg into a third dish.

Take one piece of fish and dip it into the flour, giving
it a light shake to remove excess flour and making
sure it is evenly coated, then into the egg. Toss it in the
breadcrumb mixture and set aside on a chopping board.
Repeat with the remaining pieces of fish.

Heat the coconut oil in a heavy-based frying pan. When
hot (test by dropping a few crumbs into the oil; they should
sizzle) add the fish fingers. Fry for 2–3 minutes, then turn
and cook for a further few minutes, until golden. Transfer
to a plate lined with kitchen paper to blot off any excess oil.
Season and serve with Roasted Sweet Potato Wedges (see
page 120), tzatziki (see page 57) and a green salad.

TURKEY BURGERS

50g red onions, finely chopped
Juice of 2 limes
250g turkey mince
1 medium egg
50g feta, crumbled
Pinch of paprika
Pinch of dried chilli flakes
1 tsp Lucy Bee coconut oil
Himalayan salt and ground
   black pepper

**SERVES 2 (MAKES 4 MEDIUM
BURGERS)**

Everyone loves a good burger, don't they? With added
bacon, cheese and other toppings, they're not always
the healthiest option. These turkey burgers are lovely
and light and are a great mid-week supper alternative.

Put the onions into a small bowl, add half the lime juice,
cover and leave to soak overnight in the fridge. (This will
give the burgers a delicious, zesty, sweet flavour.)

Put the turkey mince in a bowl with the egg, feta,
paprika, chilli flakes and soaked onions. Season well,
then mix together using a wooden spoon, or your hands.
Divide the mixture into three and shape into burgers,
making sure each burger is compact and holds together.

Melt the coconut oil in a frying pan over a medium
heat and, when hot, add the burgers and cook for 5
minutes, adding a dash of the remaining lime juice to the
pan. Turn and fry for another few minutes until cooked
through. If necessary, turn them again, so that they are
cooked evenly on both sides.

Remove from the heat and squeeze over more lime
juice. Season and serve with Roasted Sweet Potato Wedges
(see page 120), tzatziki (see page 57) and a green salad.

COURGETTI AND PRAWNS

300g courgettes, trimmed
200g carrots, peeled
30g Lucy Bee coconut oil
30g fresh ginger, peeled and grated
½ red chilli, deseeded and finely
    chopped
2 garlic cloves, crushed
24 raw prawns, peeled and
    deveined (tails on)
10 spring onions, very finely chopped

FOR THE DRESSING
40ml sesame oil
30g cashew nuts
25g cashew nut butter
20ml tamari sauce
Juice of 2 limes
40ml rice wine vinegar
10ml agave nectar

SERVES 2

Courgetti, or spaghetti made from courgettes, is one of those miraculous, healthy foods that I enjoy with pretty much everything. It amazes me that you can make something so delicious from a simple courgette.

Blitz the dressing ingredients together in a blender, adding a drop of water to loosen it if necessary.

Using a spiraliser, make 'spaghetti' from the courgettes and carrots. If you don't have one, cut the courgettes and carrots lengthways as thinly as possible, then across into very fine strands.

Heat the coconut oil in a wok or heavy-based frying pan, add the ginger, chilli and garlic and cook for 1 minute, stirring occasionally. Add the prawns and cook for 5 minutes or just until they turn pink (don't over-cook them), stirring every now and again. Remove from the pan.

Add the courgettes and carrots to the pan, then add the dressing, mix everything together well to coat in the dressing. Cook gently for a further 1 minute. Serve immediately, with the spring onions and prawns piled on top.

COCONUT PRAWNS

20 raw prawns, peeled and deveined
    (tails on, heads removed)
40g cornflour
1 medium egg, beaten
20g gluten-free breadcrumbs mixed
    with 40g desiccated coconut and
    a pinch each of Himalayan salt and
    ground black pepper
40g Lucy Bee coconut oil

TO SERVE
1 bunch of coriander, leaves
    chopped
Chilli Dipping Sauce (see page 175)

SERVES 2

The flavours in this wonderfully light dish really remind me of exotic holidays and gorgeous sunshine; tropical island eating at its best. You can just keep this very simple, and serve with lemon wedges.

De-vein the prawns by making a shallow cut along the length of each and removing any black line, using the tip of a knife.

Put the cornflour, egg and breadcrumb mixture into three separate dishes. One prawn at a time, dip into the cornflour, then into the egg, then into the breadcrumb mixture. Place on a plate until all the prawns are coated.

Heat the coconut oil in a frying pan until really hot (check by dropping few crumbs into the oil; they should sizzle), then add the prawns to the pan and cook over a high heat for 3–4 minutes. Turn and cook for the same time on the other side.

Serve immediately, sprinkled with chopped coriander, and with the Chilli Dipping Sauce.

SAUTÉED SQUID WITH POTATOES AND CHILLI

60g Lucy Bee coconut oil, plus a
little extra for the squid
150g red onion, finely sliced
350g cooked waxy potatoes (such
as Charlotte, Maris Peer or Jersey
Royals), cut into bite-sized pieces
2–3 garlic cloves, finely chopped
500g squid, sliced into rings
½ tsp dried chilli flakes
1 tbsp sherry vinegar
Big handful of roughly chopped
parsley and coriander
Lime wedges, to serve

**SERVES 8–10 AS A STARTER OR
4–6 AS A MAIN COURSE**

Go back five or so years and you would have
struggled to buy squid easily. Happily, most
supermarkets now sell squid — and if you have a local
fishmonger, even better! Squid always reminds me
of being on holiday, so whenever I have it at home,
those holiday memories come flooding right back.

Melt the coconut oil in a large, heavy-based frying pan.
Add the onion and gently sauté until soft, then add
the potatoes and continue to cook until the onions
and potatoes are just browning (not burnt!), stirring
occasionally.

Add the garlic and cook for 2–3 minutes, stirring often
to mix, then remove from the pan and set aside. Add a
little more coconut oil to the pan, stir in the squid and
chilli flakes and cook for 3–5 minutes, taking care not to
over-cook the squid or it will be tough.

Return the potatoes and garlic to the pan, then add the
sherry vinegar and herbs. Give everything a good stir to
combine and serve with lime wedges to squeeze over,
and a crisp Baby Gem salad.

SALT AND PEPPER SQUID

350g cleaned squid tubes
40g cornflour
40g gluten-free flour
50g Lucy Bee coconut oil
Himalayan salt and ground
black pepper
Lemon wedges or Chilli Dipping
Sauce (see page 175), to serve

SERVES 2–4

I never normally feel left out simply because I can't
eat gluten, but when I see squid on the menu in
restaurants, this soon changes, as I long to eat it.
This gluten-free version has made my life complete!

Cut the squid into thin strips. Mix the flours together in a
bowl with 5g salt and 10g pepper, then dip the squid into
the flour and give it a light shake to remove any excess.

Heat the coconut oil in a heavy-based frying pan.
When hot (test by dropping a small piece of bread into
the oil; it should sizzle), add the squid to the pan and fry
for 2–3 minutes, then turn and cook for a further couple
of minutes on the other side.

Transfer to a plate lined with kitchen paper, season
with salt and pepper and serve immediately, with lemon
juice squeezed over or with the Chilli Dipping Sauce.

BROWN RICE SPAGHETTI
WITH WILD GARLIC

500g Rizopia organic brown rice
  spaghetti
100ml Lucy Bee coconut oil
2 plump garlic cloves, finely chopped
50g wild garlic leaves (when
  in season)
Handful of chopped parsley
Himalayan sea salt and ground
  black pepper

SERVES 4

This recipe is so easy to make after a tough day at
work. Sometimes we can get a little carried away
with complex flavours or fancy ingredients, but often
I find that simpler dishes taste much nicer. This is one
of those amazing, memorable meals that combines
simple, stunning flavours with comforting spaghetti.

Heat the coconut oil in a frying pan, add the garlic cloves
and gently fry until golden but not burnt, then add salt
and pepper to taste.
  Meanwhile, cook the spaghetti according to the
packet instructions. Transfer to a warmed serving bowl.
Tip the garlicky oil onto the spaghetti, then add the wild
garlic leaves (if using), chopped parsley, mix well and
serve immediately.

BROWN RICE SPAGHETTI WITH
ANCHOVY AND TOMATO SAUCE

100g Lucy Bee coconut oil, plus a
  little extra for the greens
1 plump garlic clove, finely chopped
1 x 50g tin anchovy fillets in oil
Handful of chopped parsley, plus
  extra to serve
1 x 400g tin chopped tomatoes
500g Rizopia organic brown rice
  spaghetti
Himalayan salt and ground
  black pepper

SERVES 4

This is another fast and easy recipe. You can go from
oven to plate in just 20 minutes, and it's so intensely
satisfying and full of flavour. It tastes great on its own
but, for an added health kick, serve with broccoli or a
green salad, and a fine grating of Parmesan.

Melt the coconut oil in a large frying pan, add the garlic
and fry gently until golden brown but not burnt. Add the
anchovy fillets and their oil, which will dissolve nicely,
then the parsley, and stir for 1 minute before tipping in
the tomatoes with pepper to taste. Simmer, uncovered,
for 20 minutes.
  Meanwhile, cook the spaghetti according to the packet
instructions. Transfer to a warmed serving bowl. Pour the
anchovy and tomato sauce over the spaghetti, sprinkle
with extra parsley and serve immediately.

A satisfying quick supper that is the perfect pick-me-up after a long day. Sometimes I even make extra so that I can eat any leftovers for breakfast the next day.

EGG-FRIED WILD RICE WITH EDAMAME

80g wild rice (uncooked weight)
100g fresh edamame beans, shelled
1 tbsp Lucy Bee coconut oil
80g chard, shredded
2 tbsp pumpkin seeds
1 egg, beaten

SERVES 2

Rinse the rice, then cook according to the packet instructions. Blanch the edamame beans in boiling water until tender, then drain.

Heat the coconut oil in a wok and add the chard and pumpkin seeds. Once the chard is wilted, add the drained rice and edamame beans, mixing everything together.

Stir the beaten egg through the rice for 1–2 minutes before serving immediately.

This nutritious rice bowl topped with fresh, seared tuna is clean eating at its very best – wholesome, tasty and oh-so-satifying.

SEARED TUNA AND SESAME RICE BOWL

200g short-grain brown rice
Pinch of Himalayan salt
4 tsp nori flakes
2 tbsp Lucy Bee coconut oil
2 small, thick tuna steaks
1 avocado, peeled and sliced
½ cucumber, peeled, deseeded and
    sliced into thin batons
2 tbsp black sesame seeds, toasted
    in a dry pan
Handful of fresh coriander, leaves
    only, chopped
Pickled ginger, to serve

FOR THE DRESSING
Juice of ½ lemon
Juice of ½ orange
1 tsp manuka honey
2 tbsp tamari sauce
½ tbsp gluten-free fish sauce
1 tbsp brown rice vinegar

SERVES 4

GF   WF   DF   LF

Cook the rice in about double its volume of water with the salt for 40 minutes or until tender. Drain, transfer to a large mixing bowl and stir through the nori flakes.

Meanwhile, in a small bowl, mix the lemon and orange juice, honey, tamari, fish sauce and brown rice vinegar together to make a dressing.

Heat the coconut oil in a griddle pan to a fairly high heat, add the tuna steaks and sear for about 30–45 seconds on each side (the middle should still be pink). Remove to a board to rest for a couple of minutes, before slicing into thin pieces.

Divide the rice, avocado, cucumber and tuna slices between deep bowls. Scatter over the black sesame seeds, pour over the dressing, top with fresh coriander and serve, with pickled ginger.

SLOW COOK
WEEKENDS

This is the perfect alternative to Sunday roasts and is a real treat for family dinners come the end of the week. I just love the French-style creamy sauce, which tastes delicious with mash. Perfect for indulging!

TARRAGON ROAST CHICKEN

1 chicken, about 1.5kg
50g Lucy Bee coconut oil
½ lemon
1 large bunch of tarragon
Himalayan salt and ground
   black pepper
Chopped chives, to serve

FOR THE SAUCE
6 shallots, finely chopped
1 garlic clove, crushed
150ml white wine vinegar
200ml chicken stock (see page 181)
3 tsp Dijon mustard
60ml single cream
20g chopped tarragon leaves

SERVES 4

Preheat the oven to 200°C/400°F/gas mark 6.

Prepare the chicken for roasting by rubbing it all over with the coconut oil. Put the chicken in a roasting tray and place the lemon half and tarragon inside the chicken. Season well, transfer to the oven and roast for 1¼–1½ hours, or until the juices run clear when the thickest part of the leg is pierced with a skewer. Remove the chicken from the roasting tray and keep warm.

Place the tray over a medium heat and add the shallots, garlic and vinegar. Cook until softened, scraping any tasty bits from the bottom of the pan.

Add the chicken stock and mustard, stir together and reduce for about 5 minutes. Gradually add the cream and warm through before sprinkling in the chopped tarragon.

Carve the chicken. Serve with the tarragon sauce, sprinkled with chopped chives and accompanied by either Roast Potatoes (see page 118) or Potato and Celeriac Mash (see page 119) and steamed broccoli.

I have always used whole spices instead of ready-made mixes, as I find that mine have a real depth of flavour and I know the spices are fresh. They also work out so much cheaper. To give it a go, visit your local Indian shop and see what you can find. Just remember to use your recycled Lucy Bee jar to store your spices in.

HEALTHY CHICKEN CURRY WITH TOMATOES AND GREEN CHILLI

2 garlic cloves, peeled

Thumb-size piece of fresh ginger, peeled

1 tbsp Lucy Bee coconut oil, softened

1 large onion, chopped

2 tsp cumin seeds

1 tsp ground turmeric

1 bay leaf

1 blade of mace

2 tsp ground coriander

1 x 400g tin chopped tomatoes

2 green chillies, halved and deseeded

450g skinless chicken thighs

2 tsp dried fenugreek leaves

1 tsp garam masala (see page 181)

1 tbsp Greek yoghurt

Handful of chopped fresh coriander

Himalayan sea salt and ground black pepper

SERVES 4

GF WF

Put the garlic and ginger into a small food processor with a little water and blitz to a smooth paste.

Put the coconut oil and onion in a heavy-based, large frying pan and cook over a medium heat until golden brown.

Add the cumin seeds and stir for a minute, then stir in the turmeric, bay leaf, mace and ground coriander and cook for 1 minute. Add the garlic-ginger paste, stir and cook for a couple of minutes – enjoy the wonderful aroma!

Tip in the tomatoes and simmer for a few moments until well mixed (you may need to add a little water), then add the chillies (you can pick them out at the end if you are concerned about the heat) with salt and pepper to taste. Add the chicken, cover and cook over a low heat at a gentle bubble for 1½ hours.

Stir in the dried fenugreek and garam masala, then spoon into bowls. Top with the yoghurt, scatter over the coriander and serve with brown rice.

This is my dad's favourite dish, and pretty much everyone else loves it, too. The spices used here are great for healing and cleansing the body, while the rich flavours make it deliciously warming — perfect for cosying up with on a cold winter night.

TARKA DHAL WITH TURMERIC AND CORIANDER

FOR THE DHAL
200g red split lentils
1 litre water
4 slices of fresh ginger, peel on
1 tsp ground turmeric
1 tsp Himalayan salt
1 x 400g tin chopped tomatoes
4 tbsp fresh coriander leaves

FOR THE TARKA
3 tbsp Lucy Bee coconut oil
4 garlic cloves, sliced
½ tsp asafoetida
2 tsp cumin seeds
2 tsp ground coriander
3 green chillies, left whole or
    deseeded and sliced

SERVES 4

GF WF DF LF V

Rinse the lentils well under cold running water, then tip into a pan with the water. Bring to the boil, then skim off the scum and add the ginger slices and turmeric. Cover, leaving the lid slightly ajar, and simmer over a low heat for 1½ hours, until soft and a thick porridge consistency, stirring often to ensure it doesn't catch.

Remove the ginger slices, then add the salt and chopped tomatoes. Set aside and keep warm.

To make the tarka, melt the coconut oil in a small frying pan. Add the garlic and fry until golden. Stir in the asafoetida, cumin seeds, ground coriander and chillies, then pour into the lentil mixture. Finally add the coriander and serve with boiled rice.

At home, we call this recipe Chicken Mess, but in fact it is a fattee, which is an Arabic word for crumbled. The layers in this dish tend to be crispy flatbreads, and we make our own gluten-free versions, but shop-bought gluten-free pittas or wraps are fine here.

CHICKEN FATTEE GF WF

4 gluten-free flatbreads (see page 183)
Lucy Bee coconut oil, for brushing
    and frying
190g brown rice
2 boneless, skinless chicken breasts

FOR THE AUBERGINE SAUCE

2 medium aubergines, cut into
    2cm cubes
About 4 tbsp Lucy Bee coconut oil
2 garlic cloves, finely chopped
1 x 400g tin chopped tomatoes
1 tsp coconut sugar
1 tsp ground cinnamon
1 tbsp tomato purée
1 x 400g tin chickpeas, well rinsed
Himalayan salt and ground
    black pepper

FOR THE YOGHURT TOPPING

1 small garlic clove, peeled
Pinch of Himalayan salt
250g Greek yoghurt

TO SERVE

Handful of parsley leaves, chopped
10g pine nuts, toasted in a dry pan

SERVES 4

Preheat the overhead grill to hot, brush the flatbreads with coconut oil and grill for about 5 minutes until crisp.

For the yoghurt topping, mash the garlic to a paste with the salt, using a pestle and mortar or by squashing it on a board using the flat side of a large knife. Put the yoghurt in a bowl, add the garlic and mix until smooth.

For the sauce, melt 2 tbsp coconut oil in a large frying pan and fry the aubergine until soft, adding more oil if needed. Set aside.

Melt another 2 tbsp coconut oil in the same pan and gently fry the garlic until soft and starting to turn golden. Add the chopped tomatoes, sugar, cinnamon and tomato purée and cook gently for 15–20 minutes, adding a little water if it becomes too thick. Return the aubergine to the pan with the chickpeas and stir to mix. Adjust the seasoning and set aside. Meanwhile, cook the rice according to the packet instructions.

Slice the chicken breasts in half horizontally, by placing the palm of your hand on the breast and using a sharp knife to slice across, taking great care as you cut. Slice each halved fillet lengthways into thin strips.

Melt 1 tbsp coconut oil in the frying pan. Season the chicken, add to the hot oil and quickly fry until cooked, about 5 minutes each side. Remove and set aside.

Using one big serving dish, start with a layer of broken up crisp flatbreads then add a layer of the aubergine sauce. Add the rice, then the sauce, followed by the chicken strips. Finally, add the yoghurt topping and scatter over the parsley and pine nuts.

BARBECUE SPICED LAMB

450g lamb neck fillet, cubed or
 cut into bite-size pieces
Juice of 1–2 limes
1 tbsp ground coriander seeds
1 tbsp ground cumin
1 tsp ground cinnamon
125g Greek yoghurt
20g Lucy Bee coconut oil

SERVES 2

Don't be put off by the fact that this takes hours
to prepare – I promise that it's well worth waiting
for! The marinating time allows the spices to really
permeate the lamb, leaving the most mouth-watering
flavours imaginable.

In a glass or non-reactive bowl, combine the lamb and lime
juice, then cover, refrigerate and marinate for 2 hours.

Drain the juices from the meat and pat it dry. Mix the
spices with the yoghurt in a large bowl, and then add the
lamb, before covering and marinating in the fridge for
another 4 hours.

Remove the lamb from the yoghurt and, if cooking
on a barbecue, thread onto skewers. Brush with a
little coconut oil, then cook on the barbecue, turning
frequently to avoid burning. Alternatively, heat the
coconut oil in a large frying pan and fry the lamb, in
batches if necessary to avoid overcrowding, over a
medium to high heat, until cooked to your liking,
10–20 minutes.

Serve either just as it is, or with Roasted Sweet Potato
Wedges (see page 120), Tzatziki (see page 57) and a
green salad.

COCONUT RICE WITH CARDAMOM SEEDS

30g Lucy Bee coconut oil
200g short-grain brown rice
200ml coconut milk
200ml water
Seeds from 10 cardamom pods
Pinch of dried chilli flakes
 (optional)

SERVES 2–4

The cardamom and coconut flavours complement
each other in this rich, satisfying dish. While I love it
as an indulgent side (try it with Pan-fried Marinated
Salmon on page 76, or Chicken with Lemongrass, Lime
and Coriander on page 72), it works equally well as a
breakfast – think of it as a savoury spiced porridge!

Melt the coconut oil in a heavy-based saucepan, then
add the rice and stir to coat it in the oil. Tip in the
coconut milk, water, cardamom seeds and chilli flakes,
if using, and cook according to the packet instructions,
checking occasionally as it may need a splash more water.

For this dish, all I need to say is yum, yum, yum!
It's a great comfort food for a cold night in, especially
after a long afternoon walk. Pop it in the oven before
you go, ready for you to return home to a welcoming
and enticing aroma! If you manage not to eat it all,
then it freezes really well, which in fact helps to
intensify the flavour.

LAMB AND SPINACH KORAI

150g Lucy Bee coconut oil
550g onions, chopped
1 x 400g tin tomatoes
120ml water
50g fresh ginger, peeled and
    chopped
65g garlic cloves, chopped
900g boneless shoulder or leg of
    lamb, cut into 4cm cubes
1 tsp Himalayan salt
1 tbsp ground turmeric
1 tbsp chilli powder
1 tbsp ground cumin
1 tbsp paprika
1 tbsp ground coriander
350g spinach leaves
4 medium green chillies, stalks
    removed, left whole
50g fresh coriander, chopped
½ tbsp garam masala (see page 181)

SERVES 4

Heat the coconut oil in a large, heavy-based pan. Add
the onions and cook over a medium heat for 20 minutes,
stirring now and then, until soft and light brown.

Put the tomatoes, water, ginger and garlic into a food
processor and blend until smooth. Using a slotted spoon,
transfer the cooked onions to the paste and blend briefly
until smooth.

Return the paste to the coconut oil left in the pan, then
stir in the lamb and salt. Simmer for 30 minutes, then stir
in the turmeric, chilli powder, cumin, paprika and ground
coriander and cook until the lamb is tender, 30–45
minutes if using shoulder or 45–60 if using leg. Add a
little water now and then if the sauce starts to stick.

Put half the spinach leaves into a large pan and cook
until wilted. Blitz with a little water in the food processor,
to a smooth purée. Add to the sauce with the remaining
spinach leaves and cook for 2 minutes.

Rinse out the food processor, tip in the whole chillies
and 2–3 tbsp water and blend until smooth. Taste the
curry and add as much of this chilli purée as you wish,
depending on how hot you like it. Alternatively, put a
bowl of chilli purée on the table and allow each person
to add as much as they like.

Stir in the fresh coriander and garam masala,
then transfer to a serving dish just before serving,
with Tarka Dhal (see page 95) or Indian-style Potatoes
(see page 118).

This light but satisfying fish curry is the perfect sharing dish for an evening in with friends. Any fish with firm, white flesh works well in this dish, but for a special indulgence use monkfish fillets and even add a few extra prawns.

KERALA FISH CURRY

1 tbsp Lucy Bee coconut oil
2.5cm cinnamon stick
3 cloves
Seeds of 2 cardamom pods
5 black peppercorns
2 shallots, finely sliced
1 garlic clove, finely sliced
7 fresh curry leaves
1½ tsp ginger paste
¼ tsp ground turmeric
Good pinch of Himalayan salt
100ml water
100ml coconut milk
Squeeze of lime juice
80g green beans, topped and tailed
250g firm white flesh fish fillets, such
    as hake, haddock or pollock,
    cubed or cut into bite-size pieces

SERVES 2

Heat the oil in a non-stick pan, add the whole spices and cook until they release their fragrant aromas.

Add the shallots, give everything a stir for a couple of minutes, then add the garlic and curry leaves and soften for a few minutes until the shallots are translucent.

Stir in the ginger paste, turmeric, salt and water. Bring to the boil, then lower the heat and simmer for about 7 minutes until nicely reduced.

Add the coconut milk, squeeze in the lime juice, bring to the boil and simmer for a couple of minutes. Add the green beans and fish fillets, just covering with the sauce. Simmer gently until the fish is cooked through, 4–5 minutes.

Serve with brown rice.

You can cook this dish in an overproof casserole before transferring it to a tagine for serving. If you prefer to cook in a tagine, however, use one with a cast-iron base and place it on the hob rather than in the oven. The liquid in the tagine condenses as it hits the cooler, conical-shaped lid, but if you place the tagine in the oven the lid will heat up and so won't work in quite the same way.

AUTUMN VEGETABLE TAGINE

1 tbsp sweet paprika
½ tbsp ground ginger
1 tsp dried chilli flakes
1 tsp ground coriander
1 tsp ground cumin
Seeds of 2 cardamom pods
1 garlic clove, crushed
Juice of 1 lemon
40g Lucy Bee coconut oil, melted
2 medium carrots, cut into wedges
½ butternut squash, peeled and cut
    into bite-sized pieces
½ small cauliflower, cut into florets
1 parsnip, peeled and cut into wedges
1 aubergine, cut into 2cm cubes
1 x 400g tin chickpeas, drained
500ml hot vegetable stock
1 tbsp sun-dried tomato paste
Himalayan salt and ground
    black pepper

TO SERVE
Plain yoghurt
Chopped coriander or flat-leaf
    parsley
Gluten-free flatbreads (see page 183)

SERVES 4

Preheat the oven to 200°C/400°F/gas mark 6.

Put the spices, garlic, lemon juice and coconut oil (you may need to melt it over a gentle heat first) in a large bowl. Add salt and pepper to taste, then mix. Add the vegetables and mix thoroughly to coat.

Heat a large flameproof casserole over a medium heat, add the vegetables and sauté for a few minutes, stirring every now and then. Add the chickpeas, stock and sun-dried tomato paste, give everything a good stir, then cover and cook in the oven for about 30 minutes until the vegetables are cooked and the flavours have infused. Switch off the oven, leaving the casserole inside to rest for a few minutes, then transfer to a tagine for serving.

If using a tagine, reduce the amount of stock to 250ml and leave to simmer on the hob at the lowest possible heat for 2½ hours.

Ladle into deep bowls and serve with a spoonful of yoghurt and a scattering of herbs on top, with flatbreads alongside.

I love this alternative twist on a classic risotto.
Both wheat-free and dairy-free, this is the perfect
vegetarian comfort food.

BUCKWHEAT RISOTTO WITH
TAMARIND SWEET POTATO

3 tbsp Lucy Bee coconut oil, melted
1 medium onion, finely diced
240g buckwheat
400ml hot vegetable stock
2 large sweet potatoes, chopped into
   bite-sized pieces
1 tsp tamarind paste
Small thumb-sized piece of fresh
   ginger, peeled and grated
1 garlic clove, crushed
2 tbsp cashew nuts, finely chopped
Himalayan salt

SERVES 4

GF WF DF LF V

Heat 1 tbsp of the melted coconut oil in a heavy-based
saucepan and gently sauté the onion until soft, about
8 minutes. Add the buckwheat and stir through, coating
the grains with the oil. Add about 200ml of the hot stock,
bring to the boil, then gently simmer until the buckwheat
is tender, adding more stock as needed.

Meanwhile, in a large mixing bowl, mix the sweet
potatoes with the remaining coconut oil, tamarind paste,
ginger, garlic and a good pinch of salt. Spread out in a
roasting tray and bake in the oven for 50–55 minutes,
until crispy.

Divide the risotto between shallow bowls and top with
sweet potato and chopped cashew nuts, for a little crunch.

VARIATION

Instead of tamarind sweet potato, try ginger, chilli and
cavolo nero instead. Cook the buckwheat as directed
above then heat 1 tbsp coconut oil in a large frying pan,
add thin slices of peeled fresh ginger, from a thumb-
sized piece, 1 crushed garlic clove and 1 deseeded and
thinly sliced red chilli, with 1 tsp garam masala added
after a few seconds. Cook for 30 seconds, then add
200g shredded cavolo nero leaves, a generous pinch
of salt and a little water if necessary, to wilt, then cook
for 4–5 minutes, stirring continuously. Add 20ml white
wine or a splash of sherry vinegar to deglaze, then
remove from the heat, cover and set aside for a couple
of minutes. Stir through the buckwheat and serve.

RAINBOW FISH PIE

4 eggs (optional)
300g sweet potatoes, peeled and cut into chunks
50g Lucy Bee coconut oil
200ml milk
2 bay leaves
500g assorted fish, such as cod, haddock and salmon (including un-dyed smoked, which adds a lovely flavour)
100g raw prawns, peeled and deveined
40g gluten-free flour
2 tsp curry powder or ½ tsp ground turmeric (optional)
Bunch of parsley, leaves chopped finely
Himalayan salt and ground black pepper

SERVES 4–6

This is a favourite comfort food. It may seem a real faff to cook, but I promise, it's worth the effort. Is anything more mouth-watering than homemade fish pie?

Preheat the oven to 180°C/350°F/gas mark 4.

Place the eggs, if using, in a saucepan with cold water just covering them, then bring to the boil, turn down to a gentle simmer and cook for 10 minutes. Drain and rinse under cold water. Shell and finely chop.

Meanwhile, put the sweet potatoes in a steamer and steam for 30 minutes or until soft. Mash with 10g of the coconut oil and salt and pepper to taste.

While the potatoes are cooking, warm the milk in a heavy-based saucepan. Add the bay leaves and, working in batches of similar sized pieces, the fish and prawns. Cover and cook for 6 minutes for fillets and 4 minutes for prawns, until cooked. Remove to a dish using a slotted spoon.

When cool enough to handle, remove the skin and bones from the fish, break up any fillets into smaller pieces and place in a large mixing bowl. Strain the cooking liquid into a measuring jug and top up with milk if necessary to give 500ml. Add the chopped egg, if using.

Melt the remaining coconut oil in a pan over a medium heat, add the flour and 500ml cooking liquid and cook, stirring continuously with a whisk, for 8 minutes, until the sauce starts to thicken. Continue to stir for a further 2 minutes. Season to taste, add the curry powder or turmeric, if using, and the parsley and stir to mix. Stir the sauce gently into the fish and pour the mixture into an ovenproof dish.

Spread the sweet potato mash over the fish. Cook in the oven for 35 minutes. Serve with crushed garlic peas.

CRUSHED GARLIC PEAS

15g Lucy Bee coconut oil
1 garlic clove, crushed
500g frozen petit pois
Handful of chopped chives
Himalayan salt and ground black pepper

SERVES 4

This is a wonderful twist to liven up your peas, and is perfect with Rainbow Fish Pie.

Melt the coconut oil in a heavy-based saucepan over a medium heat, then add the garlic and fry for 1 minute. Tip in the peas, stir, then cover and cook for 5 minutes, stirring occasionally.

Stir in the chives with salt and pepper to taste. Using a potato masher, crush the peas a little.

This is one of the most delicious meals imaginable. It takes a little while to make, but is well worth the effort and packed full of flavour – a definite favourite in the Lucy Bee house.

LENTIL AND VEGETABLE MOUSSAKA

2 large potatoes, scrubbed
300ml water
60g Lucy Bee coconut oil
300g white onions, diced
200g carrots, peeled and diced
1 red and 1 yellow pepper, diced
2 garlic cloves, crushed
500g chestnut mushrooms, chopped
2 x 400g tins green lentils, drained
   and rinsed
1 tsp ground cinnamon
1 tsp ground allspice
1 tsp freshly grated nutmeg
3 tbsp tomato purée
1 x 400g tin chopped tomatoes
2 medium aubergines, sliced
Himalayan salt and ground
   black pepper

FOR THE TOPPING
10g Lucy Bee coconut oil
10g cornflour
100ml milk
1 small egg
2 tsp Dijon mustard
25g Cheddar cheese, grated
25g Parmesan cheese, grated

SERVES 6

Preheat the oven to 180°C/350°F/gas mark 4.

Put the potatoes and water in a pan, bring to the boil, then cover and simmer for 30 minutes, or until just cooked through. Strain and leave to cool before slicing into thin discs.

Melt half the coconut oil in a heavy-based saucepan. Add the diced vegetables, cover and sauté until almost softened. Add the garlic and mushrooms and continue to cook until all vegetables have softened. Add the lentils, then stir in the spices, tomato purée and chopped tomatoes. Season well and simmer for 20 minutes, stirring occasionally.

Melt the remaining coconut oil and use it to brush both sides of each aubergine slice. Place on a baking tray and cook in the oven for 5–10 minutes until soft, checking regularly. You may need to brush them with a little more oil.

Spoon a layer (about a third) of the lentils and vegetables into an ovenproof dish, about 35 x 25cm and 7cm deep, add a layer of aubergine slices, followed by a layer of potato slices. Continue layering until everything is used up, which should be three layers of each.

For the topping, melt the coconut oil in a saucepan, add the cornflour and cook, stirring, for about 2 minutes. Pour in the milk, then bring to the boil, turn down to a simmer and cook for 5 minutes, stirring continuously. Beat in the egg, mustard and salt and pepper to taste, them simmer for a further 2 minutes, continuing to stir.

Pour over the moussaka, sprinkle over the cheeses and cook in the oven for 40 minutes, until bubbling. Leave to stand for 5 minutes before serving, with a green salad.

BROWN RICE KEDGEREE

250g short-grain brown rice (or rice
of your choice)
400g mackerel fillets (or undyed
smoked haddock fillets, or salmon)
175ml water or milk
50g Lucy Bee coconut oil
175g onions, finely chopped
2 garlic cloves, crushed or finely
chopped
1 tbsp mild curry powder
Bunch of parsley, leaves chopped
Juice of 1 lemon
4–6 boiled eggs, to serve

SERVES 4–6

*The curried flavours in this kedgeree work really well
together and make the perfect comfort food after a
long day. I always make a little too much and then eat
the leftovers the next day for breakfast or lunch.*

Cook the rice according to the packet instructions and
set aside. Meanwhile, place the mackerel in a large frying
pan and add the water or milk to cover. Gently bring to
the boil, then reduce the heat and simmer for about 8
minutes. Drain, reserving the liquid. When cool enough to
handle, break into flakes and remove any skin or bones.

Heat the coconut oil in a separate pan, add the onions
and garlic and sauté until soft, before stirring in the curry
powder. Tip in the cooked mackerel and rice, then stir
in the parsley and lemon juice and continue to warm
through over a low heat.

If the mixture appears too thick, add the reserved
liquid, a little at a time, until it reaches your desired
consistency. Spoon onto plates and serve warm,
topped with a boiled egg.

BROWN RICE PASTA BAKE

Lucy Bee coconut oil, for greasing
300g organic brown rice pasta
300g Bolognaise sauce
(see page 180)
200g white sauce (see page 178)
150g Parmesan, grated
Large handful of chopped
parsley leaves

SERVES 4

*My mum makes a divine lasagne, but this is a
simplified version — it tastes every bit as wonderful
and provides all the pleasure of a lasagne, but with
a lot more ease!*

Preheat the oven to 200°C/400°F/gas mark 6. Lightly oil
an ovenproof dish.

Cook the pasta according to the packet instructions,
but leaving it slightly under-cooked (it will cook more
when baked). Drain well.

Put the drained pasta in a large mixing bowl with the
Bolognaise sauce, white sauce, 100g of the Parmesan
and the parsley, and stir together gently. Transfer to the
prepared dish, sprinkle with the remaining Parmesan and
bake in the oven for 30–40 minutes until starting to brown.

Remove from the oven and, if you can resist, let it
stand for 5 minutes before serving, with a green salad.

VEGETABLES & SIDES

CAULIFLOWER AND BROCCOLI RICE

400g cauliflower
200g broccoli
40g Lucy Bee coconut oil
Himalayan salt and ground
   black pepper

SERVES 2–4

This is a brilliant side dish that works as a delicious, low-carb alternative to rice or pasta, with curries or meats. However, I love eating this on its own too – it makes a wonderful light lunch and is packed full of nutrients and goodness.

Cut the florets from the cauliflower and broccoli and place them in a food processor. You might need to work in two or three batches, so you don't overcrowd the bowl. Blitz to grains the size of rice.

Melt the coconut oil in a heavy-based frying pan over a medium heat, then add in the cauliflower and broccoli and cook for 8 minutes, stirring occasionally to prevent sticking. Add salt and pepper to taste and serve.

CELERIAC FRIES

1 celeriac, about 1kg
30g Lucy Bee coconut oil, melted
1 tsp ground turmeric
Himalayan salt and ground
   black pepper

SERVES 3–4

Sometimes, especially on a cosy Friday or Saturday night in, you just need a plate of fries to dig into. These celeriac fries are a great alternative to potatoes and are wonderful to snack on with dips on movie nights in with family and friends.

Preheat the oven 200°C/400°F/gas mark 6.

Cut the celeriac into slices before peeling, using a sharp knife (potato peelers do not work on celeriac's tough skin), transferring the peeled slices to a bowl of cold water (to stop discolouration). Cut into fries, placing them back in the water as you work.

Put the coconut oil in a large bowl and tip in the (drained) fries. Stir through the turmeric with salt and pepper to taste, and mix again until each fry is coated evenly. If using you hands, beware that turmeric will dye your skin a nice yellow colour.

Spread evenly over a large, heavy baking sheet, leaving plenty of space between the fries, and cook for 45 minutes, or until golden and crisp. During cooking, regularly check and turn the fries.

INDIAN-STYLE POTATOES

40g Lucy Bee coconut oil
Thumb-sized piece of fresh ginger, peeled and grated
1 green chilli, deseeded and finely chopped
1 tsp nigella seeds (or cumin seeds)
½ tsp ground turmeric
1 tsp ground coriander
½ tsp garam masala (see page 181) plus extra to finish if needed
500g cooked potatoes, cut into 3cm cubes
Large handful of chopped coriander
Himalayan salt and ground black pepper

SERVES 4

The spices used in this dish help to lend a real, Indian spice sensation to the potatoes. It goes well with Lamb and Spinach Korai (see page 100), and works brilliantly with chicken or salmon too.

Heat the coconut oil in a large, non-stick frying pan over a medium heat, then add the ginger and cook for a minute or so. Add the chilli, nigella seeds and ground spices and cook for another minute.

Tip in the potatoes with salt and pepper to taste, and let a crust develop on the underside of the cubes before turning to brown the other sides; you may need to add a touch more oil to help with this process. Once beautifully browned and crisped all over, remove from the heat and stir in the chopped coriander, and extra garam masala, if preferred.

ROAST POTATOES

500g Desiree or King Edward potatoes, peeled and cut into evenly-sized pieces (leave small ones whole)
40g Lucy Bee coconut oil
Himalayan salt

SERVES 4

Who would ever think that a jar of good old Lucy Bee coconut oil could be used to make the crispest, fluffiest roasties on the planet? At family dinners, we always end up with Daisy, my Nan, Aunty Pat and Mark fighting over the crispy bits!

Preheat the oven to 200°C/400°F/gas mark 6.
Steam the potatoes until almost falling apart, about 15 minutes. To check if they are ready, lift one out – the outer edge should be fluffy. Meanwhile, put the coconut oil in a roasting tin and place the tin in the oven to heat up.

Tip the potatoes into the roasting tin and turn to coat all over in the oil. Grind a little salt over and roast in the oven for 50–60 minutes until golden and crunchy, checking and turning them every now and again, and adding more oil if needed (you can even squash some of them to create more crispy edges).

VEGETABLES & SIDES

POTATO AND CELERIAC MASH

250g celeriac
250g potatoes
20g Lucy Bee coconut oil
Himalayan salt and ground
    black pepper

SERVES 4

I love the texture that using both potato and celeriac together brings to this mash – and the coconut oil adds a delicious creaminess. Good with casseroles and chicken dishes, and you could even try adding leftovers to homemade soups.

Using a sharp knife, peel the celeriac, then cut into chunks and place in cold water to prevent discolouration.

Peel the potatoes and cut into chunks the same size as the celeriac, so that everything cooks evenly. Place the celeriac and the potato in a steamer and cook for 30 minutes, or until tender.

Put the coconut oil in a mixing bowl, with salt and pepper to taste, add the cooked celeriac and potatoes. Use an electric hand whisk to purée to a mash (or use a potato masher, but place the ingredients in a pan to mash rather than a bowl).

SWEET POTATO MASH WITH CHIVES

2 large sweet potatoes, unpeeled
Handful of chives, finely chopped
1 tsp Lucy Bee coconut oil
Himalayan salt and ground
    black pepper

SERVES 2

This is healthy comfort food at its best. At the end of a long, gruelling day, there's nothing better than putting my feet up and digging in to a huge bowlful of this mash. Try adding chilli flakes or a teaspoon of one of the flavoured oils on pages 176–177.

Preheat the oven to 180°C/350°F/gas mark 4. Bake the sweet potatoes for 40 minutes, until soft. Remove and set aside to cool for 5 minutes, then cut each in half and, using a spoon, scoop the cooked insides into a bowl.

Add the chives and coconut oil and mash until you reach your desired texture (I like it really smooth). Season well before serving.

ROASTED SWEET POTATO WEDGES

600g sweet potatoes, scrubbed
and cut into chunky wedges
2 tbsp Lucy Bee coconut oil, melted
1 tsp hot sweet smoked paprika

SERVES 4

These wonderful, crisp wedges go well with just
about every dish on the planet, or as a side with
Greek yoghurt and garlic. I sometimes sprinkle nigella
seeds over before cooking, which adds a great twist
and packs a real flavour punch.

Preheat the oven to 180°C/350°F/gas mark 4.
Toss the sweet potato wedges in the melted coconut
oil and sprinkle over the paprika. Tip into a roasting tin or
baking tray and roast in the oven for 50–55 minutes, until
crispy and delicious.

SWEET POTATO NACHOS

3 sweet potatoes, unpeeled
15g Lucy Bee coconut oil, melted
1 level tsp mild or hot paprika
(or sweet chilli)

TOPPING SUGGESTIONS
- 1 avocado, crushed and mixed
with the juice of ½ lime and
1 tsp chilli flakes
- Greek yoghurt mixed with
crushed garlic, ½ cucumber and
chopped chives
- 4 chopped tomatoes, mixed with
1 chopped red onion and a
handful of chopped parsley
- Mozzarella, torn, Parmesan,
grated, or feta, crumbled

SERVES 2

This is sure-fire evidence that you can turn any
unhealthy foods healthy. Maybe just don't add
the cheese!

Preheat the oven to 180°C/350°F/gas mark 4.
Rinse the potatoes well, then slice into very thin, even
discs, about 1mm (the thinner the better). Place in a
mixing bowl with the melted coconut oil and paprika
and turn the discs until evenly coated. Spread them out
evenly on a large baking tray, being careful not to overlap
or overcrowd them.
Cook in the oven for 35 minutes, turning every now
and again so that they crisp evenly. Reduce the oven
temperature to 140°C/275°F/gas mark 1 and, if serving
with cheese, sprinkle this over at this point. Cook for a
further 6 minutes, then remove from the oven and leave
to cool slightly before adding your chosen toppings.

VEGETABLES & SIDES

Vegetables that used to be steamed in our house are often now roasted, and roasting really adds another dimension, in sprouts bringing out a deliciously nutty and sweet flavour. For a quick lunch, sprinkle grated cheese over the roasted cauliflower and replace in the oven for 5 minutes to melt the cheese.

ROASTED VEGETABLES

ASPARAGUS

500g asparagus spears, woody ends broken off
20g Lucy Bee coconut oil, melted
Balsamic vinegar (optional, drizzle on once cooked)

BROCCOLI WITH GARLIC

500g broccoli, cut into evenly-sized florets
2 garlic cloves, crushed
20g Lucy Bee coconut oil, melted

CAULIFLOWER WITH TURMERIC

500g cauliflower, cut into evenly-sized florets
2 tsp turmeric or curry powder (see page 181 for homemade)
20g Lucy Bee coconut oil, melted

BRUSSELS SPROUTS

20g Lucy Bee coconut oil
500g Brussels sprouts, outer leaves and brown ends removed

SERVES 2

Preheat the oven to 180°C/350°F/gas mark 4.

For the asparagus, broccoli and cauliflower, toss the ingredients together well, season with Himalayan salt and ground black pepper and roast in a single layer in a baking tray for about 15 minutes, until cooked to your liking (the edges of the broccoli should be slightly brown and crispy).

For the sprouts, heat the coconut oil in a baking tray in the oven, then remove and add the sprouts. Coat well, season and roast for about 45 minutes until browned, reducing the oven temperature a little after 15 minutes.

SOUPS & SALADS

It's easy to see why soups are so popular in the cold winter months – comforting, incredibly nourishing and satisfying, and quick and easy to make. I adore all kinds of soups but have a particular soft spot for this beetroot one. Not only does its colour make it look beautiful, it's also full of nutrients and minerals, including potassium, magnesium and iron, as well as antioxidants and soluble fibre.

BEETROOT SOUP

1 tbsp Lucy Bee coconut oil,
    plus extra to finish
1 onion, chopped
2 garlic cloves, chopped
750g cooked beetroot, chopped
    (or start from raw, see Tip)
500ml hot vegetable stock
1 tbsp freshly grated horseradish
    or 2 tbsp good-quality horseradish
    sauce from a jar (optional)

TO SERVE
Greek yoghurt
Chopped chives

SERVES 4

GF   WF   VEG

Melt the coconut oil in a pan, add the onion and garlic and cook over a medium heat for a few minutes until translucent. Add the beetroot and stock and simmer, covered, for 20 minutes.

Pour into a blender and blitz until smooth. Tip back into the saucepan and stir in the horseradish, if using, and then a little extra coconut oil for a lovely, creamy finish. Pour into bowls and top with a dollop of yoghurt and some chopped chives.

TIP If cooking the beetroot from raw, leave them unpeeled and wash thoroughly. Place in a large pan of water, bring to the boil and then simmer for 30–60 minutes, depending on the size of the beetroot, until soft when pierced with a sharp knife. Leave to cool, then peel.

While many people think of soup as a winter comfort, this refreshing blend is delicious all year round. I love its unique coconut water twist, which makes the soup even more nourishing and hydrating. I sometimes sprinkle over unsweetened desiccated coconut for extra sweetness, and a spoonful of flavoured oil (see pages 176–177) adds flavour. All in all, this is the perfect meal to put a spring in your step and fight any weekday blues.

CARROT AND COCONUT SOUP

1 tbsp Lucy Bee coconut oil
400g carrots, peeled and chopped
½ butternut squash, peeled, deseeded and chopped
1 white onion, chopped
2.5cm piece of fresh ginger, peeled and grated
2 garlic cloves, chopped
1 green chilli, deseeded and sliced
¼ tsp ground cumin
¼ tsp ground coriander
¼ tsp ground turmeric
750ml hot vegetable stock
500ml coconut water
1 tbsp lime juice
Roasted pumpkin seeds or Greek yoghurt to garnish (optional)

Melt the coconut oil in a pan over a gentle heat, then add the carrots, squash and onion and cook until golden and slightly softened. Add the ginger, garlic and chilli, and cook for a further 5 minutes.

Stir in the spices, then pour in the stock and simmer for 15–20 minutes, until the vegetables are soft. Tip into a blender and blitz until smooth.

Pour the soup back into the pan and add enough coconut water to bring it to your desired consistency. Gently heat, then simmer for 2–3 minutes. Ladle into bowls, squeeze over the lime juice and top with pumpkin seeds or yoghurt, if using.

SERVES 4

GF   WF   LF   VEG

My friend Hannah's adaptation of a classic tomato soup is suitable for anyone wanting a dairy-free option. Serve with Flaxseed Bread with Anchovy and Rosemary (see page 183) and to spice things up, stir in a teaspoon of Spicy Coconut Oil Harissa (see page 177).

MY FAVOURITE TOMATO SOUP

1 tbsp Lucy Bee coconut oil
2 celery stalks, chopped
2 carrots, peeled and chopped
1 garlic clove, chopped
1 large onion, chopped
250ml hot vegetable stock or water
2 x 400g tins chopped tomatoes
A few fresh basil leaves or 2 tsp dried
2 tsp tomato purée
1 x 160ml tin coconut cream (or use 200ml coconut milk)
Himalayan salt and ground black pepper

SERVES 4

Melt the coconut oil in a heavy-based saucepan, add the celery, carrots, garlic and onion and gently sauté for 5–10 minutes until soft.

Add the stock and stir for a few minutes, then tip in the chopped tomatoes and basil, if using dried, then mix in the tomato purée and coconut cream. Bring to the boil, cover, then simmer for about 30 minutes.

Tip into a blender and blitz until smooth and creamy, then season to taste, ladle into bowls and serve, with fresh basil leaves on top, if using.

This is my twist on a good old classic soup, with cannellini beans added for goodness and creaminess. It also freezes well, so this deliciously warming soup is ideal for making in bulk.

LEEK AND SWEET POTATO SOUP

15g Lucy Bee coconut oil
350g leeks, rinsed and sliced
2 garlic cloves, chopped
500g sweet potatoes, peeled
    and chopped
1 tsp dried rosemary
1 litre hot vegetable stock
1 x 400g tin cannellini beans,
    well rinsed
Handful of chopped chives
Himalayan salt and ground
    black pepper

SERVES 4–6

Heat the coconut oil in a heavy-based saucepan, add the leeks and garlic, cover and sweat for 5 minutes.

Add the sweet potatoes, rosemary and stock, then season well with salt and pepper. Bring to the boil, cover and simmer for 15 minutes, or until the potatoes have softened.

Add the beans and heat everything together for a few minutes, then pour into a blender and blitz until smooth. Stir in the chopped chives before spooning into bowls to serve.

This is one of my absolute favourite meals as it's so full of flavour. I like to make big batches of this to freeze and reheat as a quick meal in the winter months, when nothing but a huge bowl of comforting soup will do.

LENTIL SOUP

30g Lucy Bee coconut oil
1 large onion, chopped
2 garlic cloves, chopped
1 thumb-sized piece of fresh ginger, peeled and chopped
250g red lentils
750ml hot vegetable stock
Juice of ½ lemon
Himalayan salt and ground black pepper

SERVES 4–6

Heat the coconut oil in a saucepan, add the onion, garlic and ginger and sauté for about 5 minutes, or until the onions start to colour.

Add the lentils and stock, then bring to the boil, stirring occasionally to prevent the lentils from catching. Reduce the heat to low, cover and cook for 15–20 minutes.

Add the lemon juice, then pour into a blender and blitz until smooth. Season to taste, ladle into bowls and serve.

VARIATIONS
Although this soup tastes great smooth, it's also nice with just half blended and half left as it is, to give it some texture. If you want an extra kick of flavour, add a teaspoon of turmeric, or serve with sautéed sliced garlic sprinkled over the top.

ROASTED CITRUS SALAD

1 orange, sliced into thin rounds
1 lemon, sliced into thin rounds
1 tsp Lucy Bee coconut oil, melted
½ small red onion, thinly sliced
½ fennel, shaved, plus a handful of
    fronds, to serve
120g lamb's lettuce
2 avocados, peeled and sliced
Himalayan salt

SERVES 4

When you roast citrus fruits at a high temperature they caramelise, giving a lovely texture and depth of flavour to a salad.

Preheat the oven to 220°C/425°F/gas mark 7.

In a large mixing bowl, toss the orange and lemon slices with the melted coconut oil.

Line a roasting tray with baking parchment and tip the citrus slices onto the tray. Spread out in a single layer and roast in the oven for 10–15 minutes, tossing occasionally, until caramelised. Leave to cool.

Soak the red onion slices in iced water for a few minutes (to reduce their harshness), then drain and put into a mixing bowl. Add the cooled citrus slices, fennel shavings and lamb's lettuce and toss everything together, along with a pinch of salt and the remaining melted coconut oil.

Add the avocado and toss very gently again, to bring everything together, then transfer to a serving bowl. Scatter over the fennel fronds and serve.

ROASTED AUBERGINE SALAD WITH LEMON SAFFRON YOGHURT

2 aubergines, cut into thick
    3cm rounds
2 tbsp Lucy Bee coconut oil,
    melted
Mixed radishes, finely sliced
Handful of micro herbs or
    baby leaves
Himalayan salt

FOR THE DRESSING
3 saffron threads
100g natural yoghurt
Finely grated zest and juice of
    1 lemon

SERVES 4

The robust flavours in this salad make it the perfect accompaniment to barbecued meats.

Preheat the oven to 220°C/425°F/gas mark 7.

In a large bowl, toss the aubergine rounds in the coconut oil and ½ tsp salt. Spread out on a baking tray and bake for 15–20 minutes until a deep golden colour.

Meanwhile, place the saffron threads in 3 tbsp hot water and leave to infuse for 20 minutes. To make the dressing, mix together the saffron-infused water, yoghurt, lemon zest and juice, with salt to taste.

Place the aubergine rounds on a platter, spoon over a generous amount of dressing and scatter over the radish slices and micro herbs or baby leaves.

My brother isn't a massive fan of salads, but as soon as there's halloumi in sight, his plate will be licked clean! I too love halloumi, in all manner of dishes, as I find that its slightly salty taste really lifts ingredients. Drizzled with a fresh lemon and avocado-oil dressing, this converts even the most stubborn of salad haters.

HALLOUMI SALAD

225g halloumi
1 tsp Lucy Bee coconut oil
Handful of chopped parsley

FOR THE DRESSING
30ml lemon juice
30ml olive oil
30ml avocado oil
1 tsp Dijon mustard
20ml agave nectar
1 tsp cashew nut butter
1 heaped tsp capers, chopped
Ground black pepper, to taste

TO SERVE
2 tbsp pine nuts
100g rocket
14 cherry tomatoes, halved
½ cucumber, deseeded and
    chopped into quarters
6 spring onions, finely chopped
14 green or black olives

SERVES 2

GF | WF | VEG

To make the dressing, place all the ingredients in a bottle or recycled Lucy Bee jar and shake until combined. Set aside.

Pat the halloumi dry using kitchen paper, then cut into 2cm slices. Melt the coconut oil in a frying pan over a medium heat. When hot, add the halloumi slices and cook for about 1 minute on each side, until lightly browned. Remove and set aside, then add the pine nuts for serving to the pan, lightly toast and set aside.

Arrange the salad ingredients on plates and place the halloumi slices on top. Pour the dressing over (you may have too much, in which case store in an airtight container in the fridge for up to 5 days), then sprinkle over the parsley and toasted pine nuts and serve immediately.

Kale is a nutritious superfood, which makes the perfect base for any salad. Combine with juicy figs and different coloured heritage beetroots, this salad is almost too pretty to eat.

BABY KALE WITH HERITAGE BEETROOTS, FIGS AND RICOTTA

4 heritage beetroots, a mixture
  of colours
2 tbsp Lucy Bee coconut oil, melted
4 ripe figs, cut into quarters
120g baby kale (or watercress)
200g ricotta
Himalayan salt and ground
  black pepper

FOR THE DRESSING
2 tbsp avocado oil
1 tbsp pomegranate molasses
1 tbsp cider vinegar

SERVES 4

Preheat the oven to 180°C/350°F/gas mark 4.

Wash the beetroot to remove any dirt. Coat the beetroot in the melted coconut oil and arrange on a roasting tray. Roast in the oven for 45 minutes, until the beetroot feel tender when pierced with a skewer. Set aside to cool.

Once cool, slice the beetroot into thin rounds. Place the beetroot, figs and kale in a large serving bowl. Lightly dress the salad and taste for seasoning. Add small spoonfuls of ricotta before serving.

DESSERTS

I love making this at the weekend as it feels as though you're indulging in a decadent ice cream sundae. However, it's dairy-free and about as healthy as it comes — there's the amazing health benefits you get from the potassium found in the bananas, while the gentle sweetness from the cinnamon curbs sugar cravings. The lucuma powder makes it a little sweeter and adds a butterscotch-like flavour to the dish.

BANANA AND STRAWBERRY 'ICE CREAM'

4 strawberries, for dipping

FOR THE CHOCOLATE SAUCE
2 tsp raw cacao or unsweetened
    cocoa powder
2 tsp Lucy Bee coconut oil
1 tsp almond milk

FOR THE ICE CREAM
2 medium-sized ripe bananas,
    sliced and frozen
2 strawberries
1 tsp ground cinnamon
1 tsp lucuma powder (optional)
80ml almond milk

SERVES 2

To make the chocolate sauce, put the ingredients in a small pan and gently melt, stirring until smooth and taking care it doesn't burn. Dip the four strawberries into the chocolate sauce and transfer to the fridge to set. Set aside any remaining chocolate sauce, for serving.

Put the frozen bananas into a blender with the strawberries, cinnamon and lucuma, if using. With the motor running, slowly pour in the almond milk and blend until it reaches an ice cream-like texture. You may need to stop the blender and give it a stir with a spoon until it reaches the correct, thick consistency.

Spoon into chilled bowls (to stop it melting too quickly), top with the dipped strawberries and drizzle over any remaining chocolate sauce.

Few things are more British than a spot of blackberry picking in the late summer — and this pudding is worth saving them for. On cooking, the mixture separates, resulting in a light, almost soufflé-like sponge sitting atop a lemon and blackberry sauce.

BLACKBERRY AND LEMON SAUCE PUDDING

50g Lucy Bee coconut oil, melted, plus extra for greasing
175g blackberries, fresh or frozen
150g unrefined caster sugar
Finely grated zest of 3 unwaxed lemons, and 100ml juice
3 medium eggs, separated
300ml milk
50g gluten-free plain flour, sifted
¼ tsp gluten-free baking powder
Icing sugar, for dusting

SERVES 6–8

Preheat the oven to 180°C/350°F/gas mark 4. Lightly grease a 1.5 litre ovenproof dish with coconut oil.

Spread the blackberries evenly over the base of the dish and set aside. Put the coconut oil, sugar and lemon zest in a bowl and, using an electric whisk, whisk until fluffy. Gradually add the egg yolks, lemon juice and milk, whisking all the time, until well combined.

Sift the flour and baking powder together, then add this to the mixture and whisk well until you have a smooth batter, then set aside.

Whisk the egg whites to a stiff, but not dry, peak. Stir 1 tablespoon of the whisked egg whites into the pudding mixture, to loosen, then fold in the remaining whites in two batches, taking care to keep it aerated and not to over-work. Pour this mixture into the prepared dish over the blackberries.

Bake in the middle of the oven for 40–45 minutes, or until the top is golden brown and springs back when gently touched. Remove from the oven and serve hot, with a light dusting of icing sugar, and a dollop of crème fraîche if you like.

BLUEBERRY CLAFOUTIS

20g Lucy Bee coconut oil, melted,
   plus extra for greasing
4 medium eggs
30g stevia or 75g unrefined
   caster sugar
75g gluten-free plain flour
½ tsp gluten-free baking powder
300ml milk or almond milk
150g blueberries
Icing sugar, for dusting

SERVES 6–8

Blueberries – I just can't seem to leave them alone and would eat them all day if I could! This mouthwatering clafoutis is the perfect pudding to dish up on a warm spring or summer's day.

Preheat the oven to 200°C/400°F/gas mark 6. Lightly grease a shallow 1.5 litre baking dish with coconut oil.

Put the eggs and stevia or sugar into a mixing bowl and beat until combined, light and frothy. Sift the flour and baking powder together, then beat into the egg mixture until well incorporated.

Gradually pour in the melted coconut oil and continue to beat until well blended. Slowly add the milk, continuing to beat to ensure it's mixed well.

Pour this mixture into the prepared dish and sprinkle over the blueberries. Bake in the middle of the oven for 35–40 minutes, or until well-risen and golden brown. Remove from the oven, dust with icing sugar and serve, with a little crème fraîche if you like.

RAW CHOCOLATE CHEESECAKE

FOR THE BASE
225g pecans
25g raw cacao powder
60ml raw agave nectar
50g Lucy Bee coconut oil
50g peanut butter
Pinch of Himalayan salt

FOR THE FILLING
150g cashew nuts, soaked in cold
   water for 4 hours (or for 2 hours
   in hot if you are short of time)
1 ripe avocado
30g raw cacao powder
100ml coconut milk
50g Lucy Bee coconut oil, melted
30g raw agave nectar

SERVES 8–12

Who doesn't love a cheesecake? Especially when it's raw, dairy-free and packed with nutrients. Serve this to friends and they'll never know it's good for them.

Line a 20cm round springform cake tin with baking parchment.

To make the base, put all ingredients into a blender or food processor and blitz until crumbly. Tip the mixture into the lined cake tin, spread it out evenly and press down firmly. Place in the freezer while you make the filling.

Drain the cashew nuts and blitz in a food processor until they resemble cashew butter. Add the remaining filling ingredients and whiz until smooth.

Remove the base from the freezer and spread the filling over the top. Place back in the freezer for at least 2 hours, removing 10 minutes before serving, with berries and crème fraîche, if you like. Store in the freezer.

Raspberries are one of those fruits that we always seem to have an abundance of come early summer, and this cake is a delicious way to use up any berries you have leftover from picking. Perfect for summer afternoon teas or picnics.

CHOCOLATE SPONGE WITH RASPBERRIES

100g Lucy Bee coconut oil, melted
  plus extra for greasing
4 medium eggs, separated
120ml warm water
1 tsp vanilla extract
120g stevia
130g gluten-free plain flour
2 heaped tbsp cocoa powder
¼ tsp xanthan gum
3 tsp gluten-free baking powder

FOR THE TOPPING
250g crème fraîche
1 tbsp runny honey
400g fresh raspberries

SERVES 8

Preheat the oven to 180°C/350°F/gas mark 4. Lightly grease 20cm round springform cake tin and line with baking parchment.

Place the egg yolks in a mixing bowl and beat using an electric whisk. While still whisking, slowly pour in the coconut oil, warm water and vanilla and continue until well combined.

Sift together the stevia, flour, cocoa powder, xanthan gum and 2 tsp of the baking powder. Gently fold the dry ingredients into the egg yolk mixture.

In a separate bowl, whisk the egg whites with the remaining baking powder until stiff. Carefully fold the egg whites into the cake mixture, then pour into the prepared tin. Bake in the oven for 25–30 minutes, or until a skewer comes out clean and the sponge springs back to the touch. Remove from the oven and leave to cool in the tin for 5 minutes, before turning out onto a wire rack to cool completely.

Mix the crème fraîche with the honey and spread over the top of the cooled cake, then decorate with the raspberries.

STEAMED ORANGE PUDDINGS WITH POACHED RHUBARB

60g Lucy Bee coconut oil, melted, plus extra for greasing
200g rhubarb, cut into 2cm pieces
9 tbsp agave nectar
3 medium eggs
100g stevia or 125g unrefined caster sugar
Finely grated zest and juice of 3 oranges
175g gluten-free plain flour
1½ tsp gluten-free baking powder
Pinch of xanthan gum

SERVES 6

GF   WF   DF   LF   VEG

TIP If you don't have a steamer, use a large saucepan instead. Place a dinner plate upside down on the base of the pan, then put the pudding moulds on top of the plate. Fill the saucepan with enough cold water to cover the bottom one third of the moulds. Bring to the boil, cover with a lid, then steam the puddings until cooked.

Have a steamer ready on top of the stove. Lightly grease six 150ml pudding moulds with a little coconut oil.

Place half the rhubarb into the moulds, tightly lining the bases. Pour 1 tbsp of the agave nectar into each mould, then set aside.

Put the eggs in a bowl with the stevia or sugar and whisk on a high speed, using an electric mixer, until light and creamy, 5–10 minutes. Beat in the melted coconut oil and orange zest. Sift the flour, baking powder and xanthan gum together and carefully fold this into the egg mixture, ensuring that it is well combined.

Divide the mixture evenly between the pudding moulds, making sure they are not more than three quarters full. Cover each mould with a small square of foil and fold under the rim of the moulds to seal. Place in the steamer and steam for 20–25 minutes, or until the sponge has risen and just springs back to the touch.

Meanwhile, place the remaining rhubarb in a saucepan with the orange juice and remaining agave nectar. Lightly poach for 5–10 minutes until the rhubarb is just cooked and keeping its shape, taking care not to overcook it.

Carefully remove the puddings from the steamer and remove the foil tops. Run a knife around the edges to loosen and turn them onto plates. Serve at once, with the warm poached rhubarb and some crème fraîche, if you like, and some of the rhubarb cooking juices drizzled over.

COCONUT RICE PUDDING WITH FRESH MANGO AND TOASTED COCONUT

15g Lucy Bee coconut oil
80g pudding rice
1 x 400ml tin coconut milk
400ml water
20g stevia
1 vanilla pod, split lengthways
1 mango, cut into small slices
20g coconut flakes, lightly toasted

SERVES 4

Coconut works so well with tropical fruits and flavours. This wonderfully creamy, sweet and nourishing dish is a twist on the classic rice pudding. It makes the perfect breakfast, or a luxurious pudding when nothing but a sweet treat will do.

Heat the coconut oil in a large saucepan until hot, then add the pudding rice and stir for about 2 minutes until lightly toasted and coated with oil, but not browned.

Pour in the coconut milk, water and stevia, and stir. Bring to the boil, then reduce to a simmer. Add the vanilla pod and simmer for 35–40 minutes until cooked, stirring to ensure it doesn't catch on the bottom of the saucepan.

Pour into individual bowls, top with the mango slices and toasted coconut flakes and serve.

VARIATIONS
This also works well with raspberries and flaked almonds, or blackberries and apple – try what takes your fancy!

BROWN RICE PUDDING WITH RAW FRUIT PURÉE

25g Lucy Bee coconut oil
50g coconut sugar or brown sugar
100g brown rice
500ml full-fat milk or coconut milk
1 vanilla pod, split lengthways
Mixed frozen or fresh berries, such as
    raspberries and blueberries

SERVES 4

Although I try to cut back on sugar, this creamy rice pudding is a special treat – everything in moderation! The wholegrain brown rice and full-fat milk makes this a nutritious pudding.

Preheat the oven to 140°C/275°F/gas mark 1.

Over a medium heat, melt the coconut oil in an ovenproof pan or flameproof casserole. Add the sugar and stir for a few moments until it goes syrupy, then tip in the brown rice. Stir, add the milk, stirring constantly to avoid catching. Be careful as it will bubble and froth up!

Add the vanilla pod, then cover and cook in the oven for 2 hours. Remove the vanilla pod, scraping the seeds into the rice, then give everything a good stir.

Gently blitz the berries in a blender, or mash them with a fork. Serve the rice pudding in bowls with a dollop of fruit purée in the centre of each.

Lucy Bee coconut oil works so well in place of butter in crumble toppings – I use this simple mix for loads of different fruit fillings and never get tired of it. Either stick to this recipe or try using whatever comes to hand, maybe a mixture of polenta and buckwheat flour instead of plain flour, or add desiccated coconut. My Healthy Seed Mix (see page 182) works a treat too! Any seasonal fruit works in place of the raspberries.

RASPBERRY, CACAO NIB AND COCONUT OIL CRUMBLE

450g fresh raspberries
80g chilled Lucy Bee coconut oil,
    cut into small pieces
80g gluten-free plain flour
80g coconut sugar or
    muscovado sugar
80g ground almonds
2 tbsp cacao nibs

SERVES 4

Preheat the oven to 180°C/350°F/gas mark 4.

Layer the raspberries into an ovenproof dish measuring approximately 20cm in diameter.

Put the coconut oil pieces, flour, sugar and ground almonds in a food processor and blitz to a granular consistency, taking care not to over-process to a dough. Add the cacao nibs and mix them in quickly using a spoon.

Spoon the crumble mixture over the raspberries and bake in the oven for 20 minutes until the crumble is coloured and the raspberries start to bubble through. Serve hot, with a spoonful of crème fraîche, if you like.

Gluten-free pastry is quite tricky to make and roll out, so I have to admit I sometimes get help with that bit! However, it tastes so delicious that it's most definitely worth the patience – perfect for a Friday or Saturday night treat, especially served with Banana and Strawberry 'Ice Cream' (see page 140).

STRAWBERRY AND HAZELNUT TART

FOR THE PASTRY
100g Lucy Bee coconut oil,
   plus extra for greasing
200g gluten-free plain flour
45g icing sugar
¼ tsp xanthan gum
30g roasted chopped hazelnuts
1 egg yolk
2–4 tbsp cold water

FOR THE FILLING
100g Greek yoghurt
500g crème fraîche
2 tbsp honey
400g strawberries

SERVES 6–8

Preheat the oven to 200°C/400°F/gas mark 6. Lightly grease a 23cm, loose-bottomed fluted tart tin.

To make the pastry, put the flour, icing sugar, xanthan gum and coconut oil in a food processor and process until the mixture resembles breadcrumbs. Add the chopped hazelnuts, egg yolk and 2 tbsp of cold water and mix again until the mixture comes together, adding more water if necessary. Remove and shape the dough into a round, then wrap in cling film and leave to rest for 15 minutes in the fridge.

Roll out the pastry between two sheets of cling film until quite thin (about 3mm thick) and big enough to line the tart tin. Gently peel off the top sheet of cling film and carefully invert the pastry into the tin. Remove the second sheet of cling film. If the pastry crumbles or tears, use your fingers to mould it into the gaps, as it's quite pliable. Neaten off the top edge of the pastry and chill in the freezer for 5 minutes.

Remove from the freezer, use a fork to prick the base in a few places, line with baking parchment and fill with ceramic baking beans. Bake blind for 10–15 minutes, or until the pastry is just beginning to colour. Remove the baking beans and parchment and return to the oven for a further 5 minutes until golden and cooked. Leave to cool.

Unmould the cold pastry case from the tin and place on a serving plate. Put the yoghurt, crème fraîche and honey in a bowl and mix well together. Pour into the cooked pastry case, smoothing over the top. Cut the strawberries into eighths and arrange in rounds to decorate.

CAKES &
COOKIES

This cake makes the most amazing centrepiece for afternoon teas. It looks really impressive when set on a cake stand – so much so that I bet your friends or family won't have a clue that it's so healthy. The summer berries contrast wonderfully with the rich chocolate sponge and creamy frosting.

DARK CHOCOLATE CAKE WITH DAIRY-FREE FROSTING

60g Lucy Bee coconut oil, melted, plus extra for greasing
300g almond flour
60g coconut sugar
10 tbsp raw cacao powder
4 tbsp coconut flour
2 tsp bicarbonate of soda
4 medium eggs
240ml almond milk
100g dark chocolate (at least 70% cocoa solids), melted
1 tbsp vanilla extract
Fresh raspberries, blackberries and physalis, to decorate

FOR THE FROSTING

250g cashews, soaked in cold water overnight then drained
1 tbsp lucuma powder
4 tbsp icing sugar, or more to taste
4 tbsp Lucy Bee coconut oil, melted
2 tbsp almond milk
1 tbsp vanilla extract

SERVES 8

Preheat the oven to 180°C/350°F/gas mark 4. Lightly grease two 20cm round springform cake tins and line with baking parchment.

In a large bowl, mix together the almond flour, coconut sugar, cacao powder, coconut flour and bicarbonate of soda.

In a separate bowl, and using an electric whisk, whisk together the coconut oil, eggs, almond milk, melted chocolate and vanilla until smooth and frothy.

Gently fold the dry ingredients into the wet until combined. Take care not to let too much air out of the mixture – stop as soon as the dry ingredients are just folded through. Divide between the two prepared cake tins. Bake in the oven for 20–25 minutes or until a skewer comes out clean. Leave in the cake tins for 5 minutes before turning out onto a wire rack to cool completely.

Blitz the frosting ingredients together until smooth. Taste and add more icing sugar or milk if necessary. Spread half the frosting over one of the cooled cakes, then sprinkle over half the raspberries. Place the second cake on top and spread with the remaining frosting. Top with more berries and then finish off with physalis. Enjoy, with a spoonful of crème fraîche if you like.

This is a really impressive-looking pudding to serve up to family or friends on a hot summer's day. The pineapple and passion fruit make this classic completely irresistible. Simply perfect for those summer barbecues and get-togethers.

PINEAPPLE AND PASSION FRUIT ROULADE

FOR THE ROULADE

30g Lucy Bee coconut oil, melted, plus extra for greasing
4 medium eggs
55g stevia
1 tsp vanilla extract
80g gluten-free plain flour
1 tsp gluten-free baking powder
Pinch of xanthan gum
Icing sugar, for dusting
Edible flowers, such as violas or nasturtiums, to decorate

FOR THE FILLING

150g Greek yoghurt
150g crème fraîche
4 tsp agave nectar
3 passion fruit
125g fresh pineapple, cut into very small chunks

SERVES 6–8

GF WF VEG

Preheat the oven to 180°C/350°C/gas mark 4. Lightly grease a 34 x 23cm Swiss roll tin or shallow baking tray and line with baking parchment.

Place the eggs and stevia in a bowl and whisk for 5–10 minutes on a high speed using an electric mixer until creamy, light and almost doubled in volume. Beat in the melted coconut oil and vanilla extract.

Sift the flour, baking powder and xanthan gum together, then gently fold into the egg mixture, until combined. Take care not to let too much air out of the mixture – stop as soon as the dry ingredients are just folded through. Pour into the prepared tin and bake in the middle of the oven for 12–15 minutes, or until the sponge springs back to the touch.

Leave in the tin to cool slightly. Place a flat sheet of baking parchment on the worktop, lightly dusted with icing sugar. Turn out the warm roulade onto the parchment and start to roll from the narrower end of the cake (the paper will remain inside) until you have a Swiss roll. Leave to cool completely.

Once completely cold, unroll the roulade and discard the parchment. Mix together the yoghurt, crème fraîche and agave nectar. Scoop out the seeds and pulp from the passion fruit and fold into the yoghurt mixture. Spread the fruity yoghurt over the roulade and scatter over the pineapple chunks, setting some aside for decoration.

Carefully roll up the roulade and place on a serving dish. Scatter the remaining pineapple chunks over the top of the roulade and dust with icing sugar. Decorate with edible flowers, such as violas and nasturtiums.

I've recently started using polenta more and more and I love its versatility — it tastes great in savoury meals (polenta fries just have to be tried!) and, as you can see here, it also works brilliantly with sweet ingredients too. Here it adds a lovely, crunchy texture. The perfect bake to serve with a cup of green tea on rainy afternoons, or as a dessert, with ice cream or crème fraîche.

POLENTA AND LEMON CAKE

75g unrefined caster sugar
150g Lucy Bee coconut oil, softened
4 medium eggs
1 tbsp gluten-free baking powder
100g fine polenta
200g ground almonds
Finely grated zest of 2 unwaxed
    lemons, and 20ml juice
Fresh sprigs of edible flowers,
    to decorate

FOR THE SUGAR SYRUP
Juice of 1 lemon
75g icing sugar

SERVES 6–8

GF   WF   DF   LF   VEG

Preheat the oven to 180°C/350°F/gas mark 4. Line a 20cm round springform cake tin with baking parchment.

Using an electric hand whisk, beat the sugar and coconut oil together until smooth, then add the eggs and beat until combined.

Stir in the baking powder, polenta, ground almonds, lemon zest and juice, then pour the mixture into the prepared cake tin. Bake in the oven for 35–40 minutes or until a skewer comes out clean.

Meanwhile, put the lemon juice and icing sugar for the sugar syrup in a small saucepan and gently warm until the syrup turns clear. Remove from the heat and set aside.

When the cake comes out of the oven, prick it all over with a fork and then pour the syrup over. Leave in the cake tin to cool completely before turning out onto a serving plate. Top with more sugar syrup and then finish off with sprigs of edible flowers, such as rosemary or lavender.

RAW BROWNIES

60g pecans
60g hazelnuts
140g Medjool dates, pitted
   and chopped
5 tbsp raw cacao powder
2 tbsp Lucy Bee coconut oil, melted
3 tbsp desiccated coconut
3 tbsp runny honey or maple syrup
1 tsp vanilla extract
Pinch of salt

SERVES 4–6

These brownies are easy to make, yet taste incredible. Rich and full of flavour, they're a firm favourite at home – perfect for those days where nothing but chocolate will do! As well as being extremely high in antioxidants, cacao is also known to be a mood-booster.

Line a 27 x 20cm brownie tin with baking parchment. Instead of a brownie tin, you could use a loaf tin and make thicker brownie chunks.

Blitz the nuts together in a food processor until they form small crumbs. Add the dates and process until the mixture starts to stick together.

Add the remaining ingredients and process on a high speed until it turns a lovely, gooey chocolate brown. Press into the lined tin and chill in the fridge to firm up, at least 2 hours. Turn out when chilled and slice into squares.

PARTY CUPCAKES WITH CACAO BUTTER ICING

80g Lucy Bee coconut oil, softened
80g unrefined caster sugar
2 medium eggs, lightly beaten
1 tsp vanilla extract
110g gluten-free flour
1–2 tbsp almond milk

FOR THE BUTTER ICING

65g cashew nuts, soaked in cold
   water for 2 hours
3 tbsp cacao butter, melted
2 tsp honey
½ tsp vanilla extract
10g Lucy Bee coconut oil
3 tbsp warm water

MAKES 12 CUPCAKES

When you think of birthday parties, the first thing that comes to mind is CAKE! Of course, growing up and going to friends' parties, I couldn't eat the cakes on offer and would turn up with my own little package of homemade cupcakes and other goodies.

Preheat the oven 180°C/350°F/gas mark 4. Line a 12-cup cupcake tray with paper cases.

Put the coconut oil and sugar in a mixing bowl and beat using an electric whisk. Beat in the eggs, a little at a time, then add the vanilla extract. Fold in the flour, adding the milk if the mixture is too thick, then spoon into the cupcake cases. Bake in the oven for 10–15 minutes, until golden and the tops spring back when lightly pressed. Leave to cool completely.

Place all the icing ingredients except the water in a blender and blitz until smooth. Slowly add the water until it reaches a butter icing consistency. Leave to stand in a cool place, before piping over the cupcakes.

Any leftover icing can be stored in the fridge, or frozen.

This may at first seem a little bit indulgent but it's the perfect treat after a tough week. Each ingredient is as natural and wholesome as possible — what could be better? Pears taste utterly delicious when paired with rich chocolate.

CHOCOLATE AND PEAR UPSIDE DOWN CAKE

125g Lucy Bee coconut oil, melted, plus extra for greasing
150g unrefined caster sugar
2 ripe pears, peeled, cored and cut into eighths (well-drained tinned are fine)
4 medium eggs
200g ground almonds
50g flaked almonds
25g raw cacao powder
2 tsp gluten-free baking powder
50g dark chocolate (at least 70% cocoa solids, melted, to decorate

SERVES 8

GF   WF   DF   LF   VEG

Preheat the oven to 180°C/350°F/gas mark 4. Lightly grease a non-stick 23cm square cake tin.

Mix together 50g of the melted coconut oil with 50g of the sugar, then pour the mixture over the base of the cake tin. Arrange the pears slices neatly in rows to cover the base of the cake tin, then set aside.

Break the eggs into a bowl, add the remaining sugar and beat using an electric whisk on a high speed until light and creamy in consistency, 5–10 minutes.

Whisk in the remaining melted coconut oil, then carefully fold in the ground almonds, flaked almonds, cacao powder and baking powder.

Pour the mixture into the prepared tin over the pears, ensuring the top is level. Bake in the oven for 30–35 minutes or until a skewer comes out clean. Leave in the cake tin to cool slightly before turning out onto a serving plate. Drizzle the melted dark chocolate over the pears and then serve with crème fraîche.

DOUBLE CHOCOLATE PEANUT BUTTER COOKIES

100g Lucy Bee coconut oil, melted, plus extra for greasing
90g oat flour (or gluten-free oats processed for 1–2 minutes to make a flour)
80g ground almonds
2 tbsp raw cacao powder
½ tsp bicarbonate of soda
4 tbsp stevia
50g coconut sugar
2 eggs, beaten
120g chocolate peanut butter (or regular peanut butter)
100g cacao nibs or dark chocolate chunks

MAKES 8–10 COOKIES

There are often times when all I want is to eat cookies. These peanut butter ones are much healthier than any shop-bought version and are a real treat on rainy Sunday afternoons. Just try and resist eating them all!

Preheat the oven to 180°C/350°F/gas mark 4. Lightly grease two baking trays and line with baking parchment.

Put the oat flour, ground almonds, cacao powder, bicarbonate of soda, stevia and coconut sugar in a bowl and mix. In a separate bowl, mix together the egg, peanut butter and coconut oil until smooth.

Fold the dry ingredients into the wet until just combined, then stir in the cacao nibs or chocolate chunks. Spoon a tablespoon of mixture for each cookie on the prepared baking trays, leaving room for them to spread. Bake in the oven for 8–10 minutes, or until cooked. Leave to cool, then enjoy.

OAT AND RAISIN COOKIE CHUNKS

75g Lucy Bee coconut oil
50g honey
50g coconut sugar
40g gluten-free plain flour
40g ground almonds
¾ tsp bicarbonate of soda
150g oats
½ tsp Himalayan salt
1 egg, lightly beaten
175g raisins
75g dark chocolate (at least 70% cocoa solids), broken into small pieces

MAKES ABOUT 30 CHUNKS

These delicious cookie chunks full of oat and raisin goodness are great for snacking on with friends. Quick, easy and very moreish! The only challenge is in not eating the lot... and before Jack and Tom get to them!

Preheat the oven to 180°C/350°F/gas mark 4. Lightly grease a baking tray and line with baking parchment.

Melt the coconut oil in a small saucepan over a low heat, then remove from the heat and mix in the honey and coconut sugar.

In a separate bowl, combine the flour, ground almonds, bicarbonate of soda, oats and salt. Stir in the melted coconut oil, honey and sugar mixture, then add the egg and raisins and mix well. Stir in the chocolate and combine, using a wooden spoon.

Spread the mixture onto the lined baking tray and level it out, to ensure even cooking. Bake for 12 minutes, then leave to cool completely before breaking into chunks.

CHOCOLATE GRANOLA SQUARES

FOR THE GRANOLA SQUARES

100g gluten-free oats
60g Lucy Bee coconut oil, melted
25g almonds, roughly chopped
25g mixed seeds of your choice
  (sunflower, chia, pumpkin, etc.)
1 tsp ground cinnamon
3 tbsp runny honey or agave nectar
  (optional)

FOR THE CHOCOLATE SAUCE

30g Lucy Bee coconut oil, melted
30g raw cacao or cocoa powder

MAKES ABOUT 30 SQUARES

These granola squares are the perfect sweet treat to reach for when you hit that mid-afternoon slump. You know, the kind that usually has you running for the biscuit tin.

Lightly grease and line a 34 x 20cm baking tray with baking parchment.

Mix all the ingredients for the granola squares together until well combined, then spread out on the lined baking tray, ensuring there are no gaps.

Mix the coconut oil and cacao or cocoa powder together for the sauce, then drizzle on top of the granola.

Chill in the fridge for 2 hours to set (or in the freezer for 1 hour if you're feeling impatient) before cutting into squares. Store in the fridge or freezer, otherwise the granola squares will soften and melt.

SULTANA AND PECAN MUFFINS

120g gluten-free self-raising flour
½ tsp gluten-free baking powder
40g unrefined brown sugar
1 medium egg, lightly beaten
50g Lucy Bee coconut oil, melted
100ml almond milk (see page 182)
40g pecans, broken into small pieces
120g sultanas
Finely grated zest of 1 large orange

MAKES 10 MUFFINS

Although these little muffins are gluten- and dairy-free, they are so tasty that you'd never know it. The orange zest really livens things up, and I love the way they make my house smell as they bake.

Preheat the oven to 180°C/350°F/gas mark 4. Line a muffin tray with 10 paper cases or lightly grease a silicon muffin tray.

Put the flour, baking powder and sugar in a bowl and mix. In a separate bowl, mix together the egg, coconut oil and almond milk oil until smooth. Fold the dry ingredients into the wet until just combined. Take care not to over-work the mixture or the muffins won't rise.

Fold in the pecans, sultanas and orange zest until just combined. Divide the mixture between the prepared muffin cases. Bake in the oven for 15 minutes, until springy to the touch. Leave to cool, then devour.

I have quite a sweet tooth but I don't really want to indulge in processed, sugary ice lollies and ice creams. Making these fruit lollies are the perfect fix, particularly on long, hot summer days, when all you want to do is sit back and relax with a good book.

CACAO BANANA LOLLIES

30g Lucy Bee coconut oil, melted
30g raw cacao powder
6 bananas

FOR THE TOPPINGS
Pistachios, goji berries, cacao nibs, raisins (anything you fancy!)

MAKES 12 LOLLIES

Place the melted coconut oil and cacao in a bowl and stir together until smooth and lump-free. Line a baking tray with baking parchment.

Peel the bananas, cut in half and slide onto lolly or cocktail sticks. Dunk the bananas on sticks into the melted cacao mixture. Sprinkle over your favourite topping, place on the baking tray and chill in the fridge to set, for about 1 hour.

Remove your lollies from the fridge and enjoy!

BLITZED RAW DRESSING

This dressing really brings salads to life, especially rocket with brown rice or quinoa, although it is also great with my Brown Rice Pasta Bake (see page 113). Adding avocados to a salad dressing not only makes it wonderfully creamy, but also loads it with healthy fats, which are great for glowing skin.

MAKES 4 SERVINGS

1 ripe avocado
Juice of 2 lemons
50g chopped coriander
2 tsp Dijon mustard
2 tsp agave nectar or runny honey
50ml water
Pinch each of Himalayan salt and ground black pepper

Put all the ingredients except the water, with salt and pepper to taste, into a blender, then blend together until smooth. Slowly pour in the water, with the motor running, until it reaches your desired consistency; you may need a little more water, depending on the size of the avocado.

This is best served immediately, but otherwise store the dressing in the fridge in a recycled Lucy Bee jar. Give the jar a good shake before serving.

LEMON GARLIC DRESSING

This dressing gets better with age, so store in a recycled Lucy Bee jar ready for the week ahead. If you are taking a salad into work for lunch, take the dressing in a separate container to stop your salad ending up soggy. You can add chopped fresh herbs such as parsley, chives and coriander to this dressing.

MAKES 10 SERVINGS

150g Udo's or olive oil
80ml lemon juice
2 large garlic cloves, puréed
30ml agave nectar or runny honey
30ml Dijon mustard
Pinch each of Himalayan salt and ground black pepper

Put all the ingredients, with salt and pepper to taste, into a blender bottle (vitamin shaker) and shake thoroughly, then pour into an empty Lucy Bee jar and store in the fridge.

CHILLI DIPPING SAUCE

This is a quick, healthy and easy dipping sauce for prawns or chicken, but it can also be used as a dressing for salads and vegetables. This sauce can be stored in a recycled Lucy Bee jar in the fridge ready for the week ahead. If you prefer less spice in your sauce, just leave out the green chilli.

MAKES 4 SERVINGS

1 tsp finely chopped fresh ginger
1 garlic clove, crushed
1 green chilli, deseeded and finely chopped
6 tbsp tamari sauce
Juice of ½ lemon
2 tsp agave nectar or runny honey
2 tsp sesame oil
Pinch of ground black pepper

Put all the ingredients into a blender bottle (vitamin shaker) and shake thoroughly, then pour into a recycled Lucy Bee jar and store in the fridge.

INDIAN-STYLE COCONUT OIL

Indian spices are wonderful for adding flavour to dishes; they're also great for a health boost too.

MAKES 4 SERVINGS

4 tbsp Lucy Bee coconut oil
30g fresh ginger, skin scraped, chopped
2 garlic cloves, peeled
2 red chillies, deseeded, or 1 tsp chilli powder
1 tsp cumin seeds
1 tsp ground coriander
5 cardamom pods
1 tsp ground turmeric
2 shallots, chopped
Pinch of Himalayan salt and ground black pepper

Blitz all the ingredients to a smooth paste in a food processor. Place in a recycled Lucy Bee jar and refrigerate.

SPANISH-STYLE COCONUT OIL

This oil gives food a deep, smoky flavour. Stir into soups or casseroles or use it as a sauce with your favourite meals.

MAKES 4 SERVINGS

4 tbsp Lucy Bee coconut oil
Pinch of saffron threads
1 garlic clove, peeled
1 tbsp smoked paprika
75g roasted red peppers, peeled
1 tsp ground fennel
Pinch each of Himalayan salt and ground black pepper

Blitz all the ingredients to a smooth paste in a food processor. Place in a recycled Lucy Bee jar and refrigerate.

ANCHOVY AND ROSEMARY COCONUT OIL

This is a wonderful marinade for meats, particularly lamb. The saltiness from the anchovies really brings out the rich flavours and makes for an all-round lip-smacking dinner. Add a teaspoon to soups, to liven them up, or use to fry chicken or fish.

MAKES 4 SERVINGS

4 tbsp Lucy Bee coconut oil, softened
1 x 50g tin anchovies in oil, drained
2 garlic cloves, peeled
20g fresh rosemary, leaves only
2 shallots, chopped
Finely grated zest and juice of ½ lemon
Pinch each of Himalayan salt and ground black pepper

Blitz all the ingredients to a smooth paste in a food processor. Place in a recycled Lucy Bee jar and refrigerate.

RASPBERRY CHIPOTLE SAUCE

This can be used as both a sweet and savoury sauce, although most people never think to use it in puddings. Chipotle peppers, which are smoke-dried jalapeño chillies, add a real depth of flavour and heat that I love (I sometimes add double the amount, or the whole can here!).

MAKES 12 SERVINGS

15g Lucy Bee coconut oil
1 large onion, grated
2 large garlic cloves, finely chopped
150g chipotle peppers in adobe, chopped
500g fresh or frozen raspberries
100ml cider vinegar
150g coconut sugar (or the darkest sugar you have)
Himalayan salt and freshly ground pepper

Melt the coconut oil in a heavy-based pan over a medium heat. Add the onion and cook until soft and starting to brown. Stir in the garlic and cook for a couple of minutes.

Add the chipotle peppers, stir, then add the raspberries. Cook for a few minutes until bubbling. Add the vinegar and sugar, then slowly bring to the boil. Reduce the heat and cook until reduced and thickened, about 20 minutes. Remove from the heat and leave to cool.

For a seed-free, smooth sauce (although I leave it as it is), push the mixture through a fine sieve using the back of a spoon.

When cool, transfer to a recycled Lucy Bee jar and store in the fridge.

THAI-STYLE COCONUT OIL

This is simply a flavour and aroma sensation! I stir this oil into soups or fry my favourite meats in it. It tastes great served on the side of your favourite meals for an extra boost! As it keeps really well, scale up the ingredients to make more.

MAKES 4 SERVINGS
2 red chillies, deseeded,
    or 1 tsp chilli powder
2 garlic cloves, peeled
1 lemongrass stalk, coarse outer
    leaves removed, finely chopped
30g fresh ginger, skin scraped,
    chopped
2 shallots, chopped
3 kaffir lime leaves, crumbled
Juice of 1 lime
½ bunch of fresh coriander,
    including the stalks
4 tbsp Lucy Bee coconut oil,
    softened

Blitz all the ingredients together in a food processor to a smooth paste. Store in a recycled Lucy Bee jar in the fridge.

SPICY COCONUT OIL HARISSA

Harissa is a deliciously spicy and peppery paste – sometimes extremely hot, but this version can be as fiery as you wish. You can also experiment with other spices, such as coriander. I use this as the basis for many quick and healthy suppers – it adds a real depth of flavour to chicken or fish. Try stirring a spoonful into soups for a completely different flavour sensation. It keeps well stored in the fridge.

MAKES 4 SERVINGS
2 red chillies, deseeded,
    or 1 tsp chilli powder
4 garlic cloves, peeled
100g red roasted peppers, from a
    jar (leave the chargrilled bits on)
1 tsp cumin seeds
1 tsp caraway seeds
1 tbsp tomato purée
2 tsp smoked paprika
4 tbsp Lucy Bee coconut oil,
    softened

Blitz all the ingredients together in a food processor to a smooth paste. Store in a recycled Lucy Bee jar in the fridge.

COCONUT OIL SALSA VERDE

Salsa verde is a delicious, punchy sauce made with herbs that tastes divine with meats or fish, especially on the barbecue. However, anything goes, and I also like to serve this with roasted vegetables, roasted chicken and grilled halloumi. It can be a great way of using up any green herbs you have left lurking in the back of the fridge.

MAKES 4 SERVINGS
30g parsley leaves
30g coriander leaves
1 tsp capers
1 shallot, chopped
10g dill
3 anchovy fillets in oil
Juice of ½ lemon
4 tbsp Lucy Bee coconut oil
Himalayan salt and ground
    black pepper

Put all the ingredients in a food processor, with salt and pepper to taste, and blitz to a smooth paste. Store in a recycled Lucy Bee jar.

WHITE SAUCE

My style of cooking is quick and easy, so for this white sauce all the ingredients are added at once. This way, you never get those lumps that can happen when making a roux.

MAKES 500ML
40g Lucy Bee coconut oil
40g gluten-free plain flour
500ml milk

Place all the ingredients in a large saucepan. Over a medium heat, using a balloon whisk and whisking continously, combine the oil, flour and milk to a sauce – after about 8 minutes the sauce will start to thicken. Continue cooking and stirring for a further 2 minutes.

SUN-DRIED TOMATO PESTO

My family and I are huge fans of pesto; it just goes so well with all kinds of foods, including my Goat's Cheese and Rocket Frittata (see page 62). Think outside the pasta box and use it with cauliflower pizza, courgettes, stirred into soups or spread on toast, as well as on pasta. It's a great food to have handy in the fridge.

MAKES 4 SERVINGS
100g pine nuts
80g Parmesan or any hard
    lactose-free cheese, chopped
50g Lucy Bee coconut oil, melted
125g sun-dried tomatoes
25g basil leaves
1 garlic clove, finely sliced
Juice of 1 lemon

Place the pine nuts in a dry frying pan over a medium heat and toast until golden, then tip onto a plate.
    Put the Parmesan in a food processor and blitz, then add the pine nuts and remaining ingredients, except the lemon juice, and blitz once more, until combined but still with a little texture. Pour in the lemon juice and blitz for a final 30 seconds,. Scrape into an airtight container, such as a recycled Lucy Bee jar, and store in the fridge for up to 1 week.

SUN-DRIED TOMATO HUMMUS

I adore hummus and eat it with so many things, from bread and olives to chicken, carrots, salads – the list is endless... This hummus keeps for a week in the fridge, but remove it to room temperature an hour before eating, or the coconut oil will cause it to go hard. Stir it well before serving, maybe adding a little more lemon juice.

MAKES 4 SERVINGS
1 x 400g tin chickpeas, drained
    and rinsed
20g Lucy Bee coconut oil
60g tahini
1 garlic clove, finely chopped
50g sun-dried tomatoes
50ml lemon juice
Himalayan salt and ground
    black pepper

Place all the ingredients in a food processor, with salt and pepper to taste, and blend until smooth. Serve, topped with a drizzle of olive oil, some toasted pine nuts and a shake of paprika, if you like.

BOLOGNESE SAUCE

This dish is one of my ultimate comfort foods. I love using it for a huge variety of dishes, not just with spaghetti. It's great in a shepherd's pie or lasagne and my Brown Rice Pasta Bake (see page 113). It freezes well.

SERVES 4–6

30g Lucy Bee coconut oil
200g onions, chopped
2 garlic cloves, chopped
100g celery, diced
200g carrots, chopped
500g Aberdeen Angus beef mince
1 tbsp dried mixed herbs
100ml red wine (optional)
150g sun-dried tomatoes,
    finely chopped
1 x 400g tin chopped tomatoes
Himalayan salt and ground
    black pepper

Preheat the oven to 140°C/275°F/ gas mark 1.

Heat the coconut oil in a heavy-based saucepan, then add the onions, garlic, celery and carrots and sauté for 10 minutes over a low heat, stirring occasionally, until softened and lightly coloured.

Tip in the meat and cook until browned, then stir in the mixed herbs and season well with the salt and pepper. Pour in the red wine, if using, then increase the heat and cook, uncovered, until all the liquid has evaporated.

Add the sun-dried tomatoes and tinned tomatoes, then bring to the boil, cover and cook in the oven for 2 hours until all the flavours have mingled. Alternatively, cook on the hob over a low heat.

QUICK-COOK TOMATO SAUCE

This is the perfect sauce to whip up in the evening and serve with whatever takes your fancy; it's ideal for pasta, pizzas or meatballs. Add one or more of your favourite herbs; tarragon is good if serving with chicken, or sage if serving with sausages.

SERVES 4–6

30g Lucy Bee coconut oil
6 large garlic cloves, crushed
2 x 400g tins chopped tomatoes
Juice of ½ lemon
1 tsp mixed dried herbs or 3 fresh
    thyme sprigs (optional)
Himalayan salt and ground
    black pepper

Melt the coconut oil in a heavy-based pan over a medium heat, then add the garlic and sauté until soft but not coloured.

Add the chopped tomatoes and lemon juice, then stir together. Season with salt and lots of black pepper, then stir through the herbs, if using.

Bring to the boil, then cover and simmer over a low heat for 20 minutes.

VARIATIONS

Spice it up by adding chilli flakes, cayenne pepper or fresh chilli peppers. Or stir through anchovies, chorizo or pancetta (add after the garlic, and sauté well before adding the tomatoes) or olives.

SLOW-COOK TOMATO SAUCE

If you have time to let this sauce simmer for an hour or so, it's really worth waiting for. The wine adds a twist to a classic tomato sauce, with the paprika giving it a delicious kick. I first made this with leftover wine – better for me than drinking it!

SERVES 4–6

30g Lucy Bee coconut oil
1 large onion, finely chopped
2 large garlic cloves, finely
    chopped
2 x 400g tins chopped tomatoes
1 level tsp hot smoked paprika
150ml red wine
2 tsp muscovado sugar
3 fresh thyme sprigs
Himalayan salt and ground
    black pepper

Melt the coconut oil in a heavy-based pan over a medium heat. Add the onion and sauté until softened but not browning much.

Add the garlic and cook for a few more minutes, stirring every so often so that it doesn't catch. Tip in the chopped tomatoes, paprika, wine and sugar and stir to combine. Season with salt and pepper, then add the thyme. Cover and simmer over a very low heat for 1 hour, or until reduced and thickened.

HOMEMADE CHICKEN STOCK

I like to make up huge batches of this perfect base for soups, sauces and gravies, to freeze in individual portions. Chicken soup is an ideal use for this stock, and is one of the most comforting, nourishing foods imaginable. It reminds me of duvet days snuggled on the sofa when I was ill, with my mum bringing me huge bowls of soup.

MAKES 1 LITRE
1kg chicken bones and/or carcasses
2 onions, finely chopped
4 carrots, finely chopped
2 celery stalks, finely chopped
2 garlic cloves, finely chopped
About 12 black peppercorns
2 or 3 cloves
2 dried or fresh bay leaves
A few fresh or dried thyme sprigs
A few parsley stalks

Put the chicken bones in a large saucepan, add all the chopped vegetables and cover with cold water. Bring to the boil, skimming off any scum that appears on the surface, using a spoon.
 Add the peppercorns, cloves, bay, thyme and parsley. Cover, turn down to a low simmer and cook for a couple of hours (or longer, if you wish). Strain the stock through a sieve into another saucepan or container.
 Leave to cool a little, then remove the fat by laying kitchen paper on the surface. If you wish, reduce the stock over a high heat to make it stronger.
 Portion into the required amounts and freeze when cool.

HOMEMADE CURRY POWDER

You can make your blend as hot or mild as you like; just add more chilli.

MAKES 2–3 TBSP
1 tsp cumin seeds
1 tsp coriander seeds
1 tsp mustard seeds
1 tsp fenugreek seeds
1 tsp cardamom pods
1 tsp ground ginger
1 tsp ground turmeric
½–1 tsp chilli powder, depending on how much heat you want

Put a heavy-based frying pan over a medium heat and add all the seeds, moving them around so that they don't burn. After about 1 minute, you will get a wonderful, fragrant aroma. Remove from the heat and leave to cool.
 Blitz the cooled seeds to a fine powder in a spice or coffee grinder. Mix in the remaining spices and give a final blitz. Store in a recycled Lucy Bee jar.

GARAM MASALA

For a flavour boost, add garam masala at the end of a recipe.

MAKES 2–3 TBSP
1 tbsp green cardamom pods
5cm stick cinnamon
1 tsp cumin seeds
1 tsp black peppercorns
½ tsp grated nutmeg
½ tsp whole cloves

Blitz all the spices to a fine powder in a spice or coffee grinder. Store in a recycled Lucy Bee jar.

BAHARAT SPICE MIX

This is a popular spice blend used throughout the Middle East. Baharat is the Arabic word for spices.

MAKES 2–3 TBSP
2 tsp ground black pepper
2 tsp paprika
½ tsp ground cumin
½ tsp coriander seeds
½ tsp cloves
Seeds of 3 cardamom pods

Place all the ingredients in a pestle and mortar and grind until crushed, but not too fine.

DUKKAH SPICED SEED MIX

The word dukkah means to crush or to pound in Egyptian, so is an apt name for this mix of toasted nuts and spices.

MAKES 2–3 TBSP
25g hazelnuts
1 tsp cumin seeds
1 tsp coriander seeds
2 tbsp sesame seeds
½ tsp Himalayan salt

Toast the hazelnuts and cumin and coriander seeds in a dry pan for 3 minutes. Place all the ingredients in a pestle and mortar and grind until crushed, but not too fine.

MANGO SALSA

This refreshing salsa livens up burgers, grilled meats, marinated chicken or fish. It's a great dip for sweet potato nachos.

SERVES 2–4
1 red onion, finely chopped
Juice of 1 lime
200g mango flesh
1 green chilli, deseeded and finely chopped (optional)
1 ripe avocado
Bunch of coriander, leaves chopped

Mix the onion and lime juice in a bowl and leave to marinate for 4 hours (this softens and sweetens the onions). Chop the mango and avocado into small pieces. Add with the remaining ingredients and season. Serve immediately.

ALMOND MILK

As shop-bought milks often don't contain many actual almonds, it pays to make your own.

MAKES 1 LITRE
200g almonds (soaked for 12 hours in just enough water to cover)
1 litre filtered or tap water
1 tsp runny honey or agave nectar (optional)

Drain the almonds. Transfer with the 1 litre water to a high-speed blender and blend until smooth. Strain the almond liquid through a fine sieve, muslin or clean tea towel, leaving behind the almond meal. Stir through the honey or agave, if using. Pour the almond milk into a glass jar or bottle and store in the fridge for up to 2 days.

HEALTHY SEED MIX

We now know that good fats are essential for a healthy diet, and this moreish mix is a great way to get a balanced combination of omega 3, 6 and 9 into your diet, as well as loads of trace nutrients and fibre. I use it to enrich my baking, add to my porridge or pancakes, or to scatter into my crumble toppings. It's also great on top of smoothies or yoghurt and, because it's been blitzed together, is easier to digest.

MAKES 1 JAR
250g flaxseeds
60g sesame seeds
60g sunflower seeds
60g hemp seeds
60g pumpkin seeds

Blitz all the ingredients to a smooth powder in a nut and seed grinder (or coffee grinder). Store in the fridge (to retain goodness) in a recycled Lucy Bee jar.

SALTED CHOCOLATE ALMOND BUTTER

This delicious almond butter is rich, chocolaty and incredibly tasty. It's very good for dunking strawberries or apples, but I love it so much I've even been known to sit with a jar and a spoon. You have been warned...

SERVES 4
350g roasted almonds
1 tbsp Lucy Bee coconut oil
60g dark chocolate (at least 70% cocoa solids), chopped
2 tbsp raw cacao powder
2–3 tsp honey or maple syrup
½ tsp vanilla extract
1 tsp Himalayan salt

Place the almonds in a high-powered blender and blitz to your desired consistency, scraping down the sides as you go. I like it fairly liquid, but you can have it crunchy and chunky if you prefer.

Gently melt the coconut oil and chocolate together until smooth. Add to the blender with the remaining ingredients, then blitz until combined. Taste and add more salt or honey, if needed.

Pour the almond butter into an airtight container and store in the fridge for up to 1 week – if it lasts that long!

CHOCOLATE AND PEAR JAM

This is incredibly indulgent and feels a little decadent when spread over gluten-free toast at breakfast. This delicious jam is one of my favourite chocolaty treats.

MAKES 1 JAR
3 pears, peeled, cored and diced
100–150g stevia, to taste
Juice ½ lemon
Juice ½ orange
Pinch of ground cinnamon
½ tsp Himalayan salt
1 tbsp Lucy Bee coconut oil
150g dark chocolate (at least 70% cocoa solids), chopped

Put the diced pears into a large saucepan, then stir in the stevia, lemon and orange juice and cinnamon. Place over a medium heat until it starts to simmer, then remove and pour into a bowl.

Stir in the salt, coconut oil and chocolate, and mix until the chocolate has melted. Cover and leave to cool, then place in the fridge overnight, for the mixture to thicken.

Pour the mixture back into a saucepan, bring to the boil and bubble for about 40 minutes, until it reaches 105°C on a sugar thermometer, or is a spreadable, jam-like consistency, stirring frequently so that it doesn't catch and burn. Leave to cool briefly before pouring into a jar. Leave to cool completely, then cover and store in the fridge for up to 1 week.

FLAXSEED BREAD WITH ANCHOVY AND ROSEMARY

Being coeliac, I've never been able to indulge in those freshly-baked loaves from the bakers, but here is a gluten-free loaf to enjoy. The flavours work really well together, and nothing quite beats the smell of homemade bread baking in the oven...

SERVES 4–6
225g milled flaxseed
1 tbsp baking powder
5 medium eggs
75ml water
70g Lucy Bee coconut oil, melted
6 anchovy fillets in oil, chopped
2 tbsp dried or chopped fresh rosemary

Preheat the oven to 180°C/350°F/gas mark 4. Line a baking tray with baking parchment.

Combine the flaxseed and baking powder in a mixing bowl.

In a separate bowl, beat the eggs, water, coconut oil, anchovy fillets and rosemary together, reserving a little rosemary for the top of the loaf.

Stir the wet ingredients into the dry mixture to combine, then leave to stand for about 3 minutes to thicken up. Remove the dough from the bowl and shape into a rounded, loaf-like shape. Place on the lined tray, sprinkle over the reserved rosemary and bake for 25 minutes, until a knife inserted into the centre comes out clean.

GLUTEN-FREE FLAT BREADS

Chickpea flour, also known as garbanzo bean flour, gram flour or besan, is made from ground chickpeas. Used in many countries, it's a staple ingredient in Indian and Pakistani cuisines. These simple flatbreads are naturally gluten-free, inexpensive to make and a great alternative to use with dips or curries.

SERVES 10
150g chickpea flour, plus extra for dusting
100g rice flour
¼ tsp cayenne pepper
1 tbsp finely chopped coriander
1 tsp Himalayan salt
100ml water
25g Lucy Bee coconut oil

Mix the chickpea flour, rice flour, cayenne, coriander and salt in a large bowl. Slowly pour in the water, stirring all the time until smooth. You need a nice dough that you can roll, not too sticky or too dry, so you may or may not need to add a splash more water.

Roll into a sausage shape, cut into 10 equal pieces and shape into walnut-sized balls.

Dust a work surface with chickpea flour and, using a rolling pin, roll each ball into a round, thin pancake. Keep turning and dusting them so that they don't stick.

Heat a non-stick frying pan over a medium heat and add a small amount of the coconut oil until melted. Add as many flatbreads as will comfortably fit in the pan (2 or 3) and fry for a couple of minutes on each side, until they slightly bubble and start to brown.

Add some more coconut oil and cook the remaining flatbreads.

NUTRITIONAL
INFORMATION

ALMONDS are high in heart-healthy monounsaturated fats. **Almond flour** is a good gluten-free baking ingredient and keeps cakes deliciously moist. **Almond milk** is my favourite dairy-free option to add to breakfasts and smoothies or shakes. It also happens to be a good source of protein and is rich in riboflavin, a form of vitamin B that is proven to work with other nutrients to regulate muscle strength and growth. Almond milk may even give you glowing skin and hair, thanks to its vitamin E content.

ANCHOVIES pack in a lot of flavour for such a small fish, so you only need to use a small amount. They are rich in omega-3s, which can prevent inflammation, and also in magnesium and calcium, for strong bones and teeth.

ASPARAGUS is a great way to get in your dosage of folate, vitamins A, C, E and K, and chromium.

AUBERGINES are packed with vitamins, minerals and fibre, as well as being rich in antioxidants, such as nasunin, which gives aubergine its purple colour and can protect the fats in brain cell membranes.

AVOCADO is one of the most nutritious foods you'll ever come across. Rich in healthy fats to reduce inflammation, it's high in fibre and vitamins such as K, C and E, and is also loaded with potassium. It can even help you to absorb nutrients from other plant-based foods.

BANANAS are great for your body and can aid digestion, as well as

giving you a real bounce in energy. The potassium can protect against muscle cramps.

BASIL has antibacterial as well as anti-inflammatory properties, which are great for reducing swelling, and is known to have anti-ageing properties. It is also a good way to get your vitamin A, which can protect from free radicals.

BEETROOT lends the most beautiful colour to dishes and is also incredibly good for you. It contains a unique group of antioxidants known as betacyanins (which happen to give it the vibrant colour), and it also supports the liver, purifies the blood and improves circulation.

BICARBONATE OF SODA isn't just a great home remedy for tooth whitening, insect bites and as a natural deodorant, it also neutralises stomach acid to treat heartburn and indigestion.

BLACKBERRIES have one of the highest antioxidant levels of all fruits, while they are also rich in minerals and vitamins that give a youthful glow. Blackberries are even high in vitamin K, meaning they can help to aid muscle relaxation.

BLUEBERRIES are known as a superfood and certainly pack an incredibly powerful nutritious punch. They are extremely high in antioxidants, which work to fight free radicals, and loaded with vitamin C to boost collagen formation and keep your immune system happy.

BROCCOLI is incredibly good for you. It has a blend of phytonutrients and is high in mood-boosting vitamin D. It also contains a certain flavonoid which can lessen the impact of allergies and reactions on the body. And one serving can give you 150% of your daily needs of vitamin C.

BROWN RICE is far healthier than white rice, which has been stripped of all goodness and nutrients during the refining process. It's also high in selenium, which cuts the risk of developing diseases such as heart disease, as well as manganese, which helps the body to process fats. The fibre content also helps to keep you feeling fuller for longer.

BROWN RICE PASTA, my favourite gluten-free pasta, tastes every bit as delicious as the less healthy white kind. Made from just brown rice and water, it contains the same nutrients and health benefits of rice and so is an excellent source of manganese for energy production, selenium for immune function, and magnesium, which helps to ease muscle aches and sleep problems such as insomnia.

BRUSSELS SPROUTS are a great way to get in some vitamins C and K: just one serving will give you your recommended daily allowance.

CACAO doesn't just taste delicious, it's extremely high in antioxidants, and flavanols and other components found in cacao can lower blood pressure and boost circulation. It's also a known mood-booster while the ancient

Aztecs would even use it as an aphrodisiac.

CANNELLINI BEANS are good for bulking up dishes. They have an incredibly low GI, which means they keep you feeling full for hours, giving you energy long after you've eaten. The beans are also thought to have a detoxifying effect on the body, while being super-charged with antioxidants.

CAPERS are rich in the antioxidant quercetin, which has antibacterial and anti-inflammatory properties. They also give you a healthy dose of vitamins A and K.

CARAWAY SEEDS have long been used in traditional and ancient medicines because they're packed with vitamins, minerals and goodness. They also contain essential oils, which are known to be antioxidant and also aid digestion.

CARDAMOM is deliciously fragrant and was used for centuries in Ayurvedic medicine as a treatment for mouth ulcers and digestive problems, amongst other things. It's also great for detoxifying the body as it helps to eliminate waste, and can even freshen the breath too!

CASHEWS and **CASHEW NUT BUTTER** are high in essential amino acids, heart-friendly monounsaturated fats, and minerals, particularly manganese, potassium, copper, iron, magnesium, zinc and selenium.

CAULIFLOWER is full of healthy nutrients and vitamins, including vitamins C, K and B6, and is anti-inflammatory, which helps the body to stay healthy. It is also a great source of omega-3 fatty acids and dietary fibre, and has been found to protect the lining of your stomach.

CELERIAC is full of fibre to keep your insides happy, and is also high in vitamin K to boost the bones, as well as phosphorus, iron, calcium and copper.

CHIA SEEDS contain so many nutrients for such tiny little things! They are high in fibre, calcium and heart-healthy omega-3s, and also rich in quality protein – perfect for vegetarian or vegan diets. They are also loaded with antioxidants.

CHICKPEAS, so versatile and high in nutritional value, are one of the cheapest ingredients you can buy. They are high in both fibre and protein, and have a low GI, so work as a slow-release energy source.

CHILLI FLAKES are great for adding a kick to any dish, they are also known to boost the metabolism and control appetite. They can even reduce pain, thanks to their levels of capsaicin, which can reduce pain-signalling neurotransmitters in the brain to work like a painkiller.

CHIVES are nutrient-dense and contain choline, which can help to aid sleep and relax the muscles.

CIDER VINEGAR is an ancient remedy for all sorts of ailments. It's high in acetic acid, which is antimicrobial and can kill certain bacterias.

CINNAMON is known to be a good anti-inflammatory, which can be used to fight off infections or diseases and repair tissue damage. It packs a hefty antioxidant punch, while its natural antimicrobial properties can ward off candida and fight certain strains of E Coli. As a natural sweetener, it can also stabilise blood sugar levels.

COCONUT MILK is perfect for anyone with a dairy allergy. It's also high in a medium-chain saturated fatty acid (MCFA) called lauric acid, which is both anti-viral and antibacterial. It is quickly turned into energy by the liver, meaning that it is less likely to be stored as fat by the body.

COCONUT SUGAR, from the coconut palm, is one of the most delicious natural sweeteners on the planet, adding an almost caramel-like taste to foods. Although it's relatively high in carbs and calories, it has a lower GI than some other sugars and tends to have less of an impact on your blood sugar levels. It's also far lower in fructose – a type of sugar which your body converts to fat quickly – than other sweeteners such as agave, and contains nutrients removed in refined sugar, such as iron, zinc, calcium and potassium. **Desiccated coconut** is a great way to sweeten dishes in a healthier way and I'll even use it in cakes and bakes to add flavour. It's also rich in iron and fibre.

COD is a great way of getting lean protein into your diet. It's a good source of my favourite omega-3s, known to keep your heart healthy, as well as of selenium and vitamin B12.

COFFEE is wonderful for giving you a much-needed dose of energy, as we all know, particularly first thing in the morning or before a mammoth workout.

CORIANDER can be used to treat inflamed skin, lower bad cholesterol and blood pressure, and also to strengthen the bones, owing to its calcium content.

CORNFLOUR is a good alternative in gluten-free cooking. It's high in fibre and iron, and also contains phosphorus, which supports healthy enzyme function.

COURGETTES, or zucchini, make healthy living so much easier and more exciting. They are a good source of folates, which are beneficial to the foetus during pregnancy. They're also a great way to get heart-healthy potassium into your diet, which can help to reduce blood pressure.

CUMIN, like cardamom, can be used to help with digestion, as it activates the salivary glands. It's even thought to be a natural remedy for insomnia because its vitamin complex can help to relax and induce sleep.

DATES are not only nature's sweets, they can help to relieve digestive problems such as constipation, while the minerals found in dates can help to boost bone and tooth strength. The iron content is also great for those who suffer from anaemia.

EGGS are an inexpensive source of high-quality protein. Both the white and yolk are rich in vitamins and minerals, and the yolk is full of omega-3 fatty acids. They are an excellent source of

phosphorus, selenium, vitamins A, B2, B5 and B12, as well as choline, an important nutrient for brain function.

FENUGREEK has long been used as a medicinal remedy in parts of Asia. It contains muscle-building protein, vitamin C, potassium and diosgenin.

FETA is made with sheep or goat's milk and has a strong, salty taste, which means less is more. It's a great way to get calcium into your diet, and it's also rich in vitamin B12, for red blood cell production.

FIVE-SPICE contains fennel, which can regulate digestion and is also high in folate, cinnamon to balance out blood sugars, star anise to ramp up the immune system, and antiseptic cloves and peppercorns to neutralise free radicals.

FLAXSEED is high in heart-healthy omega-3s, and also contains both soluble and insoluble fibre.

GARLIC isn't just for scaring vampires! In fact, it's full of body-loving benefits and is great for fighting off colds and flu too. It can also help to improve iron metabolism, and may help to lower blood pressure, or hypertension.

GINGER is the perfect home remedy for treating nausea and sickness – particularly good for mums-to-be – but can also help to ease symptoms of colic. Its anti-inflammatory properties also make it ideal for helping with joint or muscle pain, as well as coughs and colds.

GRASS-FED BUTTER, which is becoming hugely popular, is rich in the little-known vitamin K2. I'm a true believer in eating

GRASS-FED MEAT whenever possible. It's packed with health benefits and tends to be lower in fat than regular meat. It's also higher in conjugated linoleic acid (CLA), and heart-healthy omega-3s.

HALLOUMI is high in calcium and is also a good source of protein for vegetarians.

HAZELNUTS are naturally sweet and tasty but are also incredibly nutritious, too. They're extremely high in energy (great for a pre or post-workout snack) and monounsaturated fatty acids and essential fatty acid. As a great source of vitamin E, they're also perfect for making the skin glow.

HEMP SEEDS are wonderful for an energy boost – a perfect pre- or post-workout addition – and also high in protein.

KELP NOODLES are made from a seaweed that grows in deep waters and is popular in Asian dishes. They are high in dietary fibre, meaning they'll keep your digestive system happy and your tummy full.

KIWI FRUIT are a fantastic beautifier as they're high in vitamin C, to boost collagen and smooth out pesky wrinkles or lines. They can also help to relieve constipation and are even thought to help combat sleep problems.

LAMB, particularly grass-fed lamb, is surprisingly high in omega-3s and also omega-6 fatty acid conjugated linoleic acid (CLA), which can boost the immune system.

LEMONS are a natural immune booster and great for easing the symptoms of coughs, colds and sore throats. They increase the body's iron absorption and can give you glowing, healthy skin.

LEMONGRASS has almost never-ending health benefits; it's packed with so much goodness that it can fight plenty of chronic conditions. It's both anti-inflammatory and antiseptic and is also fantastic at detoxifying the liver. It works wonders during the cold and flu season, as it's full of antimicrobial, antioxidant properties.

LENTILS are not only a cheap addition to bulk up meals, they're also high in nutrients, and a great way for vegetarians or vegans to get their protein. They give plenty of slow-release energy, and are low in fat and calories. They can also be used to lower cholesterol, improve digestion and increase energy levels.

LIME is a citrus juice, full of vitamin C, is great at fighting off diseases and cold viruses, and can even help to give fresh, glowing skin. Lime also aids digestion and can relieve constipation.

LIVER contains very high quantities of retinol, a form of vitamin A, which can build up in the body and harm unborn babies, so should be avoided by pregnant women. For those who can safely consume liver, it's one of the most nutrient-dense foods imaginable. Not only is it a brilliant source of iron, it's also high in vitamin B12, which your body needs to create red blood cells and protein-building amino acids.

LUCUMA, a caramel-like sweetener that tastes similar to maple syrup, makes an amazing alternative to processed sugars. It has a low GI and many other health benefits too, including being high in antioxidants, fibre and anti-inflammatories.

MANGO is wonderful at helping to clear up the skin and is also high in vitamin A, which is great for eye health. It can also normalise blood sugar levels and improve digestion, thanks to a series of enzymes that can break down proteins.

MANUKA HONEY, from New Zealand, is by far the most superior of the many honeys on the market. It has antibacterial and healing properties and works wonders on fighting bugs and other nasties. It's also high in antioxidants to protect us against free radicals.

MAPLE SYRUP is a perfect option for anyone with a sweet tooth. It's high in nutrients, including magnesium, potassium, zinc and calcium.

MINT is brilliant for indigestion as it can soothe the stomach and also encourages the salivary glands to secrete digestive enzymes. It's also great for treating congestion – perfect for when you're bunged up and full of cold.

MOZZARELLA is a great source of protein, fantastic for energy levels and building muscle, but is also rich in bone-strengthening calcium and skin- and vision-loving niacin, riboflavin, thiamine, biotin and vitamin B6.

MUSCOVADO SUGAR has a really distinctive taste and is less heavily processed and refined than your standard white table sugar. Thanks to this, it retains all of the nutrients you find in cane sugar – minerals such as potassium, calcium and iron.

MUSTARD is full of health benefits, and known to ease muscle aches and pains, as well as symptoms of psoriasis

and respiratory problems. The seeds are high in omega-3s and contain phytonutrients, while the selenium and magnesium found in them have anti-inflammatory effects.

NIGELLA seeds, also called black cumin, have for centuries been one of the most widely used medicinal seeds. The ancient Greek physician Dioscorides used them to treat headaches and toothaches. They're also commonly used to aid digestion, and they can even be used as a treatment for psoriasis and eczema.

NORI is a type of seaweed that is rich in protein (some of which comes from one of my favourite superfoods, spirulina) as well as high in iron and iodine.

OATS are not only cheap to buy but they're also the perfect breakfast food as they're fantastic at fuelling the body and keeping you feeling full. Oats contain a special kind of fibre, which can lower cholesterol levels and stabilise blood sugar levels, meaning they can prevent huge spikes in blood sugar levels. They are also a great source of magnesium.

PAK CHOI, also known as bok choy, is a leafy Chinese cabbage popular in health circles because of its phytonutrients, vitamins and health-boosting antioxidants. It's also rich in potassium and iron.

PAPRIKA offers a whole host of health benefits. It's high in beta-carotene, which the body converts into the skin-loving and wrinkle-zapping vitamin A. It can even be used in homemade face masks, to reduce fine lines and leave skin glowing!

PARSLEY is rich in many vital vitamins, including C, B12, K and A, meaning that it is wonderful for keeping the immune system strong and strengthening your bones and nervous system.

PASSION FRUITS are a great way to get your vitamin C, which helps the body to fight flu-like viruses and harmful free radicals. They're also a good source of vitamin A, which is good for the eyes.

PEARS are incredibly high in fibre, which can ease digestive problems, as well as helping the body to detox. They are also a great source of vitamin C and K, and contain small amounts of potassium, calcium and iron too.

PEAS contain lots of phytonutrients with antioxidant and anti-inflammatory benefits, including some which are exclusively found in these little green gems. They also contain omega-3 fats in the form of ALAs, and plenty of vitamin E and beta-carotene for healthy skin and eyes.

PECANS are lovely and buttery in baking and are a great source of energy. They are rich in fatty acids and also contain vitamin E to rid the body of toxic free radicals and protect from diseases.

PINEAPPLE has been used for centuries to treat digestive problems and inflammation. It's high in antioxidants such as vitamins C, beta-carotene and the minerals copper, zinc and folate.

PINE NUTS are naturally sweet and delicious, but are also a good source of plant-derived nutrients, vitamins and minerals, as well as heart-healthy monounsaturated fatty acids. Their high vitamin E content makes them great for the skin.

POLENTA was once known as 'the food of the poor', but this gluten-free Italian stallion is now used in all manner of dishes. Made from ground maize, polenta is a deep yellow cornmeal and is tasty, filling and incredibly versatile.

POMEGRANATES are like nature's rubies – they just look so beautiful when added to dishes. This nutrient-dense and antioxidant-rich fruit (the most powerful of all the fruits) is also an ancient symbol of fertility and health.

POTATOES can have quite a bad reputation, with most people in health and fitness circles avoiding them. However, they can help to fight inflammation and are even known to lower blood pressure. They're also rich in vitamin B6, which can build cells and support the body's nervous system.

PRAWNS are a fantastic source of protein, and good at boosting our omega-3 levels.

PUMPKIN SEEDS are a tasty source of vitamin B and iron.

QUINOA, actually a pseudo-cereal, is a great option for anyone with a gluten intolerance, and is one of my favourite healthy carbs. It's a brilliant source of protein, fatty acids, as well as B vitamins, magnesium and calcium. It is a fibre-rich whole grain, and so wonderful for digestion.

RAISINS are a wonderful high-energy food that contain high levels of the antioxidant catechin.

RASPBERRIES are lower in sugar than many fruits but also provide you with plenty of vitamin C and other antioxidants. They are also high in flavonoids.

RHUBARB is full of nutrients. Tart and sweet, the stalks are high in vitamin K, which we need for bone health and strengthening, and minerals such as iron, copper, calcium, potassium and phosphorus. They also contain certain compounds which transform into vitamin A inside the body – a powerful natural antioxidant which helps to keep the skin healthy and fresh.

ROCKET is packed with vital phytochemicals, vitamins and minerals. It's also a wonderful source of folates and vitamin C, helping to protect from disease.

ROSEMARY is great at improving digestion and is full of anti-inflammatory and antioxidant compounds.

SAFFRON is one of the world's most highly-prized spices and is loved for its colour, intense flavour and medicinal properties. It's high in plant-based chemical compounds that have antioxidant and disease-preventing qualities, while it also has therapeutic uses as an antiseptic and anti-depressant. It's also been used for treating everyday problems, including asthma, coughs and colds, insomnia, PMT and heartburn.

SAGE offers an array of health benefits. Its rosmarinic acid can act as both an anti-inflammatory and antioxidant and is even thought to enhance memory.

SALMON is packed full of goodness and body-loving properties. It's high in omega-3s and is also a good source of skin-boosting vitamin E. It's also a wonderful source of lean protein for muscle building and repair, and also contains essential amino acids and vitamins A, D B6 and B.

SESAME OIL and **SESAME SEEDS** are packed with magnesium as well as zinc, which is essential for producing collagen to smooth out wrinkles and plump up the skin. Sesame is also one of the best sources of calcium on the planet. **Tahini**, a paste made from sesame seeds, is one of my favourite ingredients and I love to add it to dressings and sauces for an added health boost.

SHALLOTS generally have a higher mineral content than your typical onion. They are also high in antioxidants, which are released when the shallot is crushed or sliced, and contain iron to boost energy, cell regrowth, healing and metabolism.

SMOKED HADDOCK is a fantastic source of lean protein, so is great for keeping you full and satisfied. It's also loaded with minerals, including magnesium, potassium, iron, calcium and selenium. Be sure to buy your smoked haddock free from the yellow food dye often added to make it look more attractive.

SPINACH is one of those leafy greens that just keeps on giving, full of body-loving boosters. I like to add handfuls to all sorts of meals – including green smoothies – since it is so high in vitamin C and full of anti-inflammatories and antioxidants. Adding spinach to your diet is also a great way to dose up on vitamin K, which is good for strong bones. It's also a wonderful source of energy, contains folic acid, and can improve the quality of the blood, thanks to its high iron content.

SQUID adds a lean form of protein to your diet, and are extremely high in copper, which is essential for helping the body to absorb iron.

STEVIA is a natural sugar substitute, and is about three times as sweet as ordinary sugars.

SULTANAS come from red grapes, so are high in antioxidants such as resveratrol, which has been found to be anti-inflammatory, as well as fighting against certain cancers and lowering bad cholesterol.

SUNFLOWER SEEDS are a good way to get folate in pregnancy.

SWEET POTATOES are one of the healthiest foods on the planet. They're an excellent source of vitamin C and are also rich in vitamin D, which boosts the immune system, helps to raise energy levels, and can even make us feel happier. Their high vitamin E content is good for fresh, youthful skin, and their beta-carotene is antioxidant and antiviral.

TARRAGON contains plenty of phytonutrients, antioxidants and vitamin C to help boost health and prevent disease. The compounds found in this delicious herb are also known to stimulate appetite.

THYME is a good source of vitamins C and A, iron, manganese, copper and dietary fibre. It's also believed to fight bacteria found in foods.

TOFU is an ideal vegan source of protein as it contains all eight essential amino acids. It is also high in iron and calcium, as well as manganese, selenium, phosphorous, magnesium and zinc.

TOMATOES are incredibly nutrient-dense and contain an array of nutrients and antioxidants, including alpha-lipoic acid, which helps to convert glucose to energy, and lycopene, which helps to protect against free radicals. They are also a good source of vitamins A and C, as well as folic acid, making them the perfect staple for pregnant women.

TURKEY is very lean and the high levels of protein will keep you full for hours. It also contains selenium.

TURMERIC is a super-spice and a traditional remedy for all sorts of ailments, including depression, bloating, jaundice, menstrual pain, toothache, bruises and even colic in young babies. It contains curcumin, a powerful antioxidant that has strong anti-inflammatory effects to ward off colds and flu.

WALNUTS are packed with omega-3 fatty acids – great for glowing skin and hair.

Firstly a huge thank you to my mum, Natalie, and dad, Phil. Without their hard work and dedication, none of this would have been possible. They are the reason I have such a passion for healthy eating. They made growing up a coeliac easier and more enjoyable with all the homemade gluten-free dishes they rustled up over the years. I'm sure my sister, Daisy, and brother, Jack, will agree.

The Lucy Bee team all worked so hard together to compile the delicious recipes for this book. It was a group effort and the hard work really did pay off. Petrina Grint – Thank you for being there 24/7. Your organisation made a crazy busy time so much easier. I'm so lucky to work with someone who cares so much. Meg Phizacklea – It's always enjoyable working with people you love spending time with. I can't wait for many more fun times ahead. Sam Hadadi – You have a real talent in the kitchen and I'm so thankful that you let us share some of your recipes. Karl Brown, The Trainer – aka Mr Positive – You bring sunshine on a rainy day! Hannah Grint – Spicing up the timeline on twitter! Thanks for all you do on social media and I'm looking forward to what's to come. Sarah Pearce – Baking at its best. I loved all the recipes you contributed and I'm sure everyone else will too. Ash Buckingham – I enjoyed spending time with you in the kitchen, coming up with mouth-watering recipes on a sunny day! I learnt so much. Thanks Uncle Ash! Jim Kinloch and Edward Palmer – Thanks for continuously coming up with new ideas as we move forward. Sorry your Big Boy BBQ Ribs didn't make it in this time! Indra Clementson – Thank you for introducing us to coconut oil so many years ago! I really don't know where we'd be without it.

To Quadrille Publishing, thank you for this incredible opportunity. It's a dream come true! To all the girls who worked so hard to make this book look better than we could ever have imagined. Thank you again for your hard work, music choices and laughter while working together – it was a great time. So thanks to Lisa Pendreigh, Katherine Keeble, Emily Lapworth, Ria Osborne, Hannah Hughes, Emily Jonzen, Jenna Leiter, Poppy Mahon, and Holly Bruce.

Finally, Lucy Bee Lovers – Where would we be without all of you? Due to your consistent loyalty and love for the brand you inspire us every day! Thank you x

Lucy Bee